Wicked
VERMONT

Wicked VERMONT

THEA LEWIS

THE
History
PRESS

Published by The History Press
Charleston, SC
www.historypress.com

First published 2018

Manufactured in the United States

ISBN 9781467138741

Library of Congress Control Number: 2017963926

For Mom. Thanks for making life interesting.

CONTENTS

FEARLESS, FLAMBOYANT AND FREE

The National Statuary Hall inside the United States Capitol in Washington, D.C., is filled with figures that were contributed by the individual states to honor people who are important to their history. It's a majestic collection, made up of one hundred statues, two per state. Vermont's statues were both donated in the late 1800s. Artist Preston Powers's likeness of Jacob Collamer was the most recent, added to the collection in 1881. Collamer, a Vermonter by way of Troy, New York, attended the University of Vermont and held honorary degrees from UVM and Dartmouth. A lawyer, he served four terms in the Vermont House of Representatives and was humble enough to be surprised when he was elected to an assistant judgeship on the Vermont Supreme Court, a role he bowed out of after serving for almost a decade.

Vermonters sent him to the U.S. House of Representatives in 1842, and he later served as postmaster general under President Zachary Taylor. Well spoken, an acclaimed speech writer, passionately antislavery and a supporter of President Abraham Lincoln, the guy was the whole enchilada where the embodiment of Vermont history and ideals is concerned.

Then there's the other statue: an imagining of Ethan Allen, contributed in 1876 by artist Larkin G. Mead. It's the logical choice, the romantic choice. But is it the right choice?

I know Ethan Allen is right up there when it comes to Vermont folk heroes. He's considered our founding father, the guy who, in 1775, surprised sleeping British troops to capture New York's Fort Ticonderoga with his militia, the Green Mountain Boys, and infamous traitor Benedict Arnold. Some lore would have you believe that he could strangle a bear with his bare hands or outrun a deer. In his own memoir, he wrote of once biting the head off a tenpenny nail to escape his captors. He's the man most Vermonters point to when they think of our state's independence, the standard bearer for our brave, modern Vermont National Guard. But while Ethan Allen was a lot of things, many of them noteworthy, putting his image, quite literally, on a pedestal at our Capitol reminds me of a quote from Gregory Maguire's *Wicked: The Life and Times of the Wicked Witch of the West*: "Where I'm from, we believe in all sorts of things that aren't true…we call it history."

The statue at the Capitol re-creates Allen as large-eyed, strong-jawed and curly-haired. But since he lived before Joseph Nicéphore Niépce took the very first photograph back in 1826, Ethan Allen may have been like the fine print descriptions for merchandise that looks too good to be true—"Not exactly as shown." Etchings, paintings and statuary run the gamut from matinee-idol handsome to a disheveled "morning after" look. One homage depicts an almost cartoonish image with what some of my media friends used to call "a face for radio."

History seems to agree that Ethan Allen was big and strong, with a personality to match—attributes mentioned by fans and detractors alike. The Ethan Allen Homestead in Burlington, Vermont, relays that he was more than six feet tall, rare in those days. His own younger brother, Ira, who near as I can tell spent much of his life struggling with an inferiority complex because of his older brother's oversized personality, wrote, "The real facts were that for a few days he could out travel me, in the wilderness.…He was a man of firm constitution, larger and stronger than myself."

He was smart, too. Born in Litchfield, Connecticut, the eldest of eight children of Joseph and Mary Baker Allen, he had a philosophical nature and was on track to attend Yale until his studies were derailed by his father's death. Was it bitterness at missing out on furthering his education, at getting a chance to prove his brilliance, that made Ethan Allen need to constantly be at the head of the line when someone was passing out attention?

Whether he arrived at his personality thanks to nature or nurture, accounts of his adult life paint him as savvy and well spoken but also as a drunken, flamboyant windbag. Even admirers have written that he was "belligerent" and "confrontational." He was known to be a hard partier and a brawler. Author Willard Sterne Randall wrote in *Ethan Allen: His Life and Times* that nearly every story about Allen had some connection to a tavern.

Ethan Allen, National Statuary Hall, Washington, D.C. *Courtesy the Library of Congress.*

And then there was the fact that he couldn't stop philosophizing—about liberty, but also about God and mankind. He left Salisbury, Connecticut, where he operated an iron forge after annoying just about everyone in town with his deist ways. (Apparently all is forgiven, as there's an Ethan Allen Street in Salisbury, and he's got a museum there, too.) He was even kicked out of Northampton, Massachusetts, for his rowdy behavior. After he moved, with his brothers, to fertile southern Vermont, purchasing land claimed by

Governor Benning Wentworth as part of the New Hampshire Grants, he handled any challenge to his property rights by tarring and feathering people and burning their houses. When a doctor in Bennington named Samuel Adams encouraged fellow citizens to repurchase their properties to obtain the New York rights, Ethan Allen and his posse of Green Mountain Boys tied him to a chair and strung him up outside a local tavern until he learned to keep his mouth shut. There's every indication that for Ethan Allen, brother Ira and others of their ilk, the Revolution wasn't just about freedom. It was about real estate, greed and fame, too.

Have I mentioned that the Allen brothers weren't your everyday homesteaders? They purchased *sixty thousand acres* of land in Vermont and formed the Onion River Land Company, a move they expected would pay off big-time. Ira was particularly interested in Burlington because of its waterway, Lake Champlain. Thinking of controlling it, and the lake trade that went with it, made the brothers see the colonial equivalent of dollar signs. (I'm picturing a guy in frontier garb riffling a stack of bills, hollering, "Make it rain!")

The website All Things Liberty (allthingsliberty.com) puts Benedict Arnold at the top of the list for "Biggest Jerk of the Revolution," but Ethan Allen makes a decent showing. Author Gary Shattuck said that while Allen may not be the *most* despicable, he should at least be rated high on the list. "[A]ggrandizing, mean, and endlessly insufferable," he said, noting that Allen bullied peaceful New York settlers and couldn't get elected to a leadership position in the Vermont militia he was famously part of. There was also his impulsive, failed capture of the British-controlled city of Montreal, Canada, months after his storming of Fort Ti, that landed him in prison for three years and almost got him executed, an incident he later romanticized. Shattuck concluded his opinion by saying, "Allen angered many at all levels and was, by and large, pretty much a jerk."

I'm sure, during the Revolution, there were plenty of obnoxious, alcohol-steeped blowhards fighting for the cause. But it was Allen whom Lemuel Hopkins, a physician and poet of the time, was thinking about when he composed the following poem, a scathing bit of satire that paints a picture of the man and his reputation:

> *LO, Allen 'scaped from British jails,*
> *His tushes broke by biting nails,*
> *Appears in Hyperborean skies,*
> *To tell the world the Bible lies.*

See him on green hills north afar
Glow like a self-enkindled star,
Prepar'd (with mob-collecting club
Black from the forge of Beelzebub,
And grim with metaphysic scowl,
With quill just plucked from wing of owl)
As rage or reason rise or sink,
To shed his blood, or shed his ink.
Behold inspired from Vermont dens
The seer of Antichrist descends,
To feed new mobs with hell-born manna
In Gentile lands of Susquehanna,
And teach the Pennsylvania quaker,
High blasphemies against his Maker.
Behold him move, ye stanch divines!
His tall head bustling through the pines;
All front he seems like wall of brass,
And brays tremendous as an ass;
One hand is clinch'd to batter noses,
While t' other scrawls 'gainst Paul and Moses.

"A self-enkindled star." I couldn't have said it better. Don't get me wrong, though. I know the capture of Fort Ticonderoga was a significant turning point in the fight for America's freedom. Even though the military conflict was more of a siege of some mostly sleepy people by the Green Mountain Boys, led by Allen and Benedict Arnold, (both of whom, afterward, tried to parlay the raid into as much positive PR as they could), the artillery confiscated was transported to Boston to hold off the British there. So, job well done.

And while Ethan Allen managed to escape execution for his Montreal antics, he served more than two years in prison courtesy of the British (don't feel too bad; admirers came to visit him bearing food and gifts), leaving others to fight the Revolution without him. Upon his return home, he was given the rank of major general in the Vermont militia.

In 1777, Vermont was an independent republic with statehood still years away, and Ethan and Ira Allen were concerned that the Continental Congress would not recognize Vermont. Hedging their bets in hope of exerting some control over their destiny, they began, in 1780, playing both sides against the middle as part of secret negotiations with Canadian governor general Frederick Haldimand. They put up a front, seemingly interested in reconciling Vermont with the British while waiting for the state's political fate to unspool. Unfortunately, the British weren't planning to endlessly play the waiting game. After a series of delays on the part of the Allens, Haldimand jumped the gun, issuing a proclamation outlining plans for Vermont to join the British fold. There was a hostage taken, bloodshed and, inevitably, suspicion on the part of some Vermonters regarding just what those Allen boys were up to *now*.

Fortunately, we have Ethan Allen's writings to document some of his shenanigans. There was a narrative of his time in captivity, made all the more impressive because he embellished it based on a play written by a forty-six-year-old Philadelphia man with the colorful pen name "Dick Rifle." However historically inaccurate, the play portrayed Allen as one of the great American heroes of his time. Why not embrace it?

Ethan Allen wrote pamphlets and letters about political matters but is perhaps best known for the book *Reason: The Only Oracle of Man*, originally co-written with friend and mentor Thomas Young. Their discussions on the topic of deism began in the 1760s, and their work on the book started

Green Mountain Boys in council. Illustration by Lossing-Barritt. *Courtesy Wikimedia Commons.*

Ethan Allen Homestead. *Courtesy the Library of Congress.*

around 1765. After Young died in 1777, Allen approached his widow to ask for the manuscript, which Allen rewrote. It languished for some time with a printer who didn't have the guts to touch it, but it was finally published in 1784 by Haswell and Russell of Bennington. Interestingly, the manuscript doesn't in any way acknowledge Young's contribution, and I hope what happened next was a case of him putting a posthumous whammy on his young protégé. Of the five hundred copies printed, only two hundred were sold, and a fire at the publishing company ruined the bulk of the books that remained. Haswell called it divine intervention and ordered the rest burned too.

Ethan Allen's final years were spent farming his fertile Intervale lands in Burlington. We know he died on February 12, 1789, two years before Vermont joined the Union, but we're not sure how. Some say our most famous Green Mountain Boy suffered a stroke crossing frozen Lake Champlain, but others say that his death was caused, at least in part, because he fell from his sleigh in a drunken stupor.

Ethan Allen Monument, Greenmount Cemetery, Burlington, Vermont. *Courtesy Roger Lewis.*

And get this: Ethan Allen was a slippery rascal even in death. Nobody is really sure whether his remains rest under his giant granite statue (at thirty-five feet, the tallest in the state) at Burlington's Green Mount Cemetery or in another grave site on the grounds—or perhaps (and I'm betting on this one) another location entirely, having been dug up by cronies and reinterred on a piece of land with some personal significance, probably during a big drunken party. That would have been right up his alley. If you visit, check out Ira's monument nearby, tiny by comparison. Poor Ira—he had reason to feel insecure.

Ethan Allen believed in reincarnation and used to claim while hefting a bottle fireside that he would return after his death as a powerful white stallion. Weirdly enough, people who travel near the Intervale lands where he once made his home have reported seeing a beautiful white steed rampaging around in the tall grasses in the early hours of the morning. As the sun comes up and the mists clear, the equine spirit disappears.

Should you ever wish to raise a glass to Ethan Allen, you might want to try a stonewall (sometimes called a stone fence), the drink he liked to knock back at his beloved hangout the Catamount Tavern in old Bennington, Vermont. It's a few ounces of rum topped off with hard apple cider. Some suggest muddying it up with ginger beer and lime wedges, but why mess with a drink that was, well, revolutionary?

EMBARGO SCHMARGO

*W*hat can you say about a guy who made his living carting contraband goods to Canada? You can say a lot, especially if the guy in question is Gideon King.

Gideon King, technically Gideon King Jr., was a force to be reckoned with in the Burlington of the late 1700s and early 1800s. His family were some of the first proprietors, or landowners, in Burlington, and King was probably the most entitled among them.

Boastful, competitive and (some thought) greedy, he shaped Burlington's history and our country's maritime history with it. He's the guy who bought decommissioned navy ships from the Revolution on the cheap and brought them to Burlington's harbor, refurbishing them for future use. Unfortunately, the boats were filled with rats, which were also introduced into the harbor. Gross.

King was called the "Admiral of the Lake," and not in a nice way, as King wasn't a guy who played nice. He owned taverns and hotels, and he controlled traffic on the lake. He was an important man, and everyone knew it because he handled every aspect of his life "like a boss." At one point in time, he either owned or owned interest in just about every boat in Burlington's harbor, along with the docks and stores to which the goods from those ships were transported. He was a mule when crossed, determined to have his own way and not above bending the rules or breaking the law to turn a situation to his favor.

In 1807, in an attempt to forestall a war and persuade France and Britain to respect America's neutral rights, Thomas Jefferson decided to impose an embargo on foreign trade. It ended up being a yearlong lesson in futility. The embargo was a nightmare that put people out of work and gouged the economy. Smuggling reached new heights, especially in Vermont and Canada.

Because Gideon King was a businessman who made much of his fortune on the lake, he wasn't about to let a little thing like an embargo put a kink in his hose. With all those ships at his disposal, he became a smuggler on a very large scale, moving potash, timber, whiskey, coffee and more along the watery superhighway that was Lake Champlain. He even moved furs for tycoon John Jacob Astor.

Customs agents had a rough time with the smuggler. Jabez Penniman, a local doctor, was appointed by the feds to a position as a customs agent because he was well liked and well respected in the region that is now Chittenden County. He encountered Gideon King moving stealthily on the lake one night in one of his ships with a hull painted black with tar so it was harder to spot out there in the moonlight. He and his men boarded King's vessel, and Penniman warned King that the jig was up and that if

Trade embargo political cartoon. *Courtesy the Library of Congress.*

he didn't stop his smuggling, it was going to go bad for him. King replied that he allowed no man to tell him how to run his business—why should the president be any different?

Still, King was warned, so he became more careful. He hadn't been doing his smuggling alone. He employed plenty of young men, many of them Irish and a bit rough around the edges. The Irish did not have the best reputation in early 1800s America, so if something went wrong, it was no surprise, and no skin off King's nose. It's rumored that King used these same Irish fellows to create a network of tunnels from his wharf on the waterfront into the town, to his property, to the properties of his relatives and underneath the homes of other lake captains. During that time, it paid to keep your friends close and enemies closer. Smugglers, even top-drawer ones like King, had more than the law to contend with. What was to stop another smuggler from stealing your ill-gotten gains?

While many of the reports of smuggling were sensationalized (Penniman himself wrote that even though the smugglers were "as thick as locusts and as troublesome as gnats…you may consider…three parts out of four of the reports in circulation are false…no man is killed—no man is hurt—no boat is run away with—King has not drowned me yet."), there were incidents of violence and even death on the water and on dry land. The case of the *Black Snake* and the *Fly* was one of those.

The *Black Snake* was a smuggling vessel, decked out as the name implies—covered with tar, completely black in the moonlight. When Jefferson's embargo was in full swing, it was as stealthy as they came.

In August 1808, someone leaked to the customs officials that the *Snake* would be carrying a stash of potash, important in the production of glass and soap, to Canada. So, they sent a twelve-oar boat christened the *Fly* to intercept it. They caught up with the *Snake*, tucked into the Winooski River near property that was once part of Ethan Allen's homestead. It was empty, the crew having fled to dry land, but not before taking their weapons. Customs agent Jabez Penniman had believed, when disbursing information to the *Fly*'s commander, that the *Black Snake* crew was only *lightly* armed. Sadly, that was not the case. The ship was loaded with firepower, including a lethal seventy-five-pound, nine-foot-long cannon called a "wall gun."

Now, it wasn't unusual for those smugglers to carry two or three gallons of rum for the crew, so both the law and the smugglers had probably refreshed themselves that morning with the seafaring version of a "breakfast of champions."

The *Black Snake*'s crew was armed and watchful as the *Fly* crew split up to board their ship, stationing lookouts on the shore. The smugglers—tired, cranky, drunk and more than a little nuts over the whole thing—opened fire with their cannon, which was crammed full of some pretty ghastly ammunition. The *Fly*'s commander, Lieutenant Daniel Farrington, was critically wounded, and three other men were killed nearly instantly.

The smugglers began to lose it—running, I imagine, like actors in an old *Keystone Cops* short—because by this time they realized that the situation has turned not just bad but really, *really* bad, and it was entirely possible their goose was cooked.

The owner of the land to which they'd retreated, Jonathan Ormsby, was one of the men killed. He was a farmer who fought in the Revolutionary War, and although later reports tried to paint him an innocent bystander, he was one of the people who had given advance intel to the government and added to the confusion by shouting commands at young Lieutenant Farrington during the melee. The smugglers were eventually rounded up by militiamen and locked up in the hoosegow on Courthouse Square in the center of Burlington.

The public cried out for swift punishment, and they got it. A special grand jury was convened, and the men were brought to court in a span of just ten days. They were Samuel Mott of Alburg; Cyrus Dean and Josiah Pease of Swanton; three Highgate boys, William Noaks, Slocum Clark and Truman Mudgett; David Sheffield of Colchester; and Francis Ledyard of Milton. Mott and Dean were convicted of murder, but Mott got off on a technicality—that is to say, they didn't hang him, but he still had to face the music. His sentence was reduced to manslaughter, and his punishment was to stand in the stocks for one hour, to be properly jeered at, I guess, and submit to fifty lashes while tied to the whipping post, a pine tree on the south side of what is now Burlington's City Hall Park. After that, he was to serve ten years hard time in prison.

Most of the other men got similar sentences, but Noaks and Clark escaped, making it clear that the jail needed to be reinforced. They were never heard from again, and it was suspected they met with some type of vigilante justice.

In the end, Cyrus Dean took the fall (pun intended) as the only guy to hang. He was just twenty-eight and newly married with a small child, which might have garnered some sympathy if he hadn't rubbed people the wrong way. He was the only one of the accused who struggled with captors when he and his cohorts were nabbed, and he rattled his jailers by making them look bad when he nearly managed to escape out a window even though his hands and feet were bound at the time. All throughout the trial, he professed his innocence, but the motion to have his judgment amended failed. He was sentenced to a gallows built especially for him at the western edge Burlington's Elmwood Cemetery.

He was supposed to hang on Friday, October 28, 1808, but received a stay of execution from the governor. There was some confusion, causing him and others to assumed that his sentence would be commuted. The city, believing this to be true, tore down the original scaffold, which had to be rebuilt at an additional expense when it was discovered the governor hadn't had been lenient, just very, very busy.

At noon on Friday, November 11, 1809, a huge crowd estimated at ten thousand people had gathered in Burlington to witness the State of Vermont's first official execution. Cyrus Dean was brought to the courthouse for the ultimate exit interview with Reverend Truman Baldwin of Charlotte, who begged him to confess his sins. His pleas fell on deaf ears. Dean was brought to the gallows, where people had assembled from far and wide to watch what was, in those days, a rare entertainment. It would be the first and last hanging of that magnitude inside the limits of the city of Burlington.

Witnesses said they had never seen a man about to die look so unconcerned. His coffin had been placed, conveniently, just below the gallows platform. A noose was placed around Dean's neck, and Reverend Baldwin made one last attempt to get him to repent. He spat on the coffin, looked out at the crowd, said he wasn't guilty and pulled his hat down over his eyes. He "swung" at three o'clock in the afternoon.

The story of the *Black Snake* and the *Fly* has captured the imagination of many a Vermonter. Here's writer, composer and folksinger Pete Sutherland's ode the "*Black Snake* Affair":

> *A storm of war is brewin', oh see the lightning flash*
> *Tho the woolen mills of England, they still call out for ash*
> *In Tom Jefferson's embargo, the king of England's blind*
> *For he cannot tell Canadian ash from our Green Mountain kind*
>
> CHORUS: *And its ashes, potashes, with ashes laden down*
> *The wily boat the Black Snake for Montreal is bound*
> *So pass the word downriver from town to mountain town,*
> *For a smuggler's grimy dollar, all the forest will come down!*

Now hear this, Dr. Stoddard, your hand you soon must fold
There's a Fly within my Customs House, a twelve-oar cutter bold
Along the broad lake highway, this Fly will soon take wing
And Mudgett and his smuggler boys will feel the deadly sting
Oh tell me, Dr. Penniman, why do you raise alarm?
For tho we heed no Customs House, we mean your men no harm
Your soldiers cruise the broad lake, to stop our trade they try
But were they not born Green Mountain boys the same as you or I?
(CHORUS)

That long hot first of August, in the year Eighteen-oh-eight
With a jug of rum in a sheltered bay the Black Snake's men did wait
At nightfall to set sail again, the eastern shore to gain
Then up the Onion River, there Joy's landing they'd attain
And it was half a day behind her rowed hard the cutter Fly
On old North hero's wooded shore a handkerchief she spied
"Take care, Lieutenant Farrington where the river weaves and winds,
Follow the trail of onions and the Black Snake there you'll find"
(CHORUS)

"Lieutenant," cried the helmsman, "I see her 'round the bend
This snake be ripe for taming, her evil's at an end,"
So Farrington, he jumped aboard—from the beach there came a yell:
"Now the man who lays a hand on her, I'll blow his brains to hell!
Come on my boys—parade yourselves—you're cowards to a man!
The Black Snake she is boarded and its we must make a stand!"
"Your blood upon this river!" it was then the smuggler's cry
And the battle soon was joined between the Black Snake and the Fly
(CHORUS)

Now across the wide Winooski, the muskets loudly sang—
And for murdering three customs men, one smuggler has to hang
One smuggler he'll be hanged and the rest to prison gone
Tho they're sure to gain their pardon with this war a-comin' on
So raise your glass to smugglers, for they help small towns survive
And now the lake's alive with snakes—the potash business thrives
Of the reputations ruined, not one can be regained
But who with a boat and a bottle of rum might not yet do the same?
(CHORUS)

Gideon King House. *Courtesy Roger Lewis.*

I've got a spooky side story about Gideon King and a crazy peek back in time at what a consummate businessman he was. Gideon King's old haunt at 115 St. Paul Street, now the American Flatbread Burlington Hearth, has long been rumored to be haunted, with eyewitness accounts spanning more than six decades. King reportedly built the place in the first decade of the 1800s. He rented out half the space and used his half for "storage." The basement has been a particular hot spot throughout the years, and at least one restaurant manager in the building's history prohibited female servers from going alone down to the basement for supplies after multiple reports of young women being pinched, pushed or having their hair yanked by invisible forces.

Water turning on and off in the restrooms, unexplained noises and shadows and large objects like holiday wreaths being heaved across the room by an unseen hand are just some of the things people have experienced in the restaurant. A tenant in an apartment upstairs claimed that whenever he and his girlfriend would argue, his lights would flicker and his laptop would begin playing the same Spanish-language YouTube video, although neither of them had initiated it.

American Flatbread Company. *Courtesy Roger Lewis.*

We know that Gideon King hated the embargo, but how did he feel about taxes? While falling down the rabbit hole of history via my subscription to newspapers.com, I learned that way back on December 8, 1800, a lot was leased to Gideon King's father for an annual lease rental fee of $60. Eight years later, on May 17, 1808, while ship's captain, businessman and smuggler Gideon King was administering his father's estate, he somehow got the city to agree that if he paid $1,000 *up front*, it would eliminate the $60 fee for 999 years. Seriously, either the city needed money very badly or Gideon King was the Obi-Wan Kenobi of the nineteenth century.

The parcel was on land designated School Lot 165, 103 acres that extended from the northern boundary of what is now UVM's East Woods near Proctor Avenue, south to the Hadley Road neighborhood. It was Burlington land before the city was incorporated in 1865, but it was redistricted to become a western boundary of South Burlington.

Because of King's agreement, there are folks on White Place, a street just across Route 7 from the Queen City, who pay taxes on their house but *not* on their land. And neither will anyone who buys their property until May 2807.

THE END OF THE LINE

I believe in curses. They're a great way to administer payback
for, at the very least, keep people in line. But visiting a curse on your
great-grandkids seems going a little too far.

In 1806, a man named William Hayden moved to the town of Albany,
Vermont, when it was still called Lutterloh, after Colonel Henry Emannuel
Lutterloh, who was deputy quartermaster general under George Washington.
With him were his wife, Silence, whom he'd married in Massachusetts in
1798, and his mother-in-law, a quick-minded woman with lots of cash
named Mercie Dale. In order to get the family off to a proper start, Mercie
paid for the land and their new home, the first frame house in the village.

William was an entrepreneurial type, and he had big plans. He wanted
to start a business, and he asked his mother-in-law to help him with the
financing. She agreed to the loan and watched as her son-in-law became
a successful man with a variety of ventures. Unfortunately, William
neglected for years to pay Mercie back the money he owed. He took a
job as a surveyor, but thanks to his lust for property, he began accepting
plots of land instead of a paycheck. Real estate wise, he was fat—his bank
account, not so much.

So, William began to ask Mercie for more and more money, and the
widow became uncomfortable with the arrangement. He hadn't even paid
her the first loan she'd extended. She was put out, to say the least, but had
her daughter and grandchildren to think of, so she continued to accept the
situation for what it was.

During that time, there was a trade embargo going on, enacted by Congress against France and Great Britain. With smuggling rampant on Lake Champlain and through "the Notch," a popular mountain trail for bringing contraband in and out of Quebec by land, William somehow managed to become a customs agent on the Canadian border. When Mercie heard a rumor that William was smuggling cattle to boost his cash reserves, she was furious. William had money—he just preferred to spend it on a whatever he wanted rather than pay her what she was owed. Harsh words were spoken, and she moved out of the family home.

A kind neighbor, Sally Rogers, took the woman in, but all the stress from worrying and arguing about money caused Mercie to become ill. Now bitter and suspicious, she became obsessed with thinking William had poisoned her. On her deathbed, during a visit from her daughter, Silence, Mercie cursed the Hayden family, saying, "The name will die in the third generation, and the last to bear the name will die in poverty." She refused to be buried in the family plot, saying she would not, in death, lie next to any of the Haydens. She chose instead to be interred on her neighbor's land.

William still had a tavern and a textile mill, but cut off from Mercie's cash flow, he watched them slip away. It was all downhill from there. William lost everything he had and was forced to run away to Canada to escape his debts. He ended up in prison in Montreal, eventually moving to Farnsworth, New York, where he did die penniless, as his mother-in-law predicted.

William and Silence had five sons, but they all died before they reached adulthood except one. That was William Hayden II, born in 1800, who was called Will. Will stayed in Albany and became a railroad contractor, building lines between Canada and Nashua, New Hampshire.

In 1854, he built Hayden House, situated between Wylie Hill Road and Route 14's crossing of the Rogers Branch of the Black River. The place was a two-and-a-half-story Greek Revival building, five bays wide and four bays deep.

It had two parlors and a suspended dance floor in the ballroom for extra bounce; people could step-dance to their heart's content without destroying the ceilings below. An oval staircase rose from the center hall to the second floor.

In the design were four chimneys and multiple units that appeared to be fireplaces but were really furnace registers with grilled openings framed by ornate mantels that were painted to resemble marble. The furnace was designed to accommodate logs six feet in length.

Hayden House. *Courtesy National Register of Historic Places.*

Hayden House staircase during renovations. *Courtesy National Register of Historic Places.*

The house was surrounded by Italianate gardens and more than thirty fruit trees. In William Hayden's day, people considered it the finest house they had ever seen. It is rumored, though facts have not been found to support the theory, that Hayden kept Chinese workers that he used like slaves in quarters in the basement of the house, letting them out to work the gardens and fields on his property. People said the place was a monument to himself and that he'd been heard to say, "We'll show these fools in Albany what money can do."

Eventually, thanks to some misstep on his part, William lost his railroad gig and had to start a new career from the ground up. He opened a mercantile and enjoyed some success, but bad fortune seemed determined to haunt him. He and his wife, Azubah, never happily married, were constantly at each other's throats. One night, on his way home, he was thrown from his wagon and seriously injured. He later lost his eyesight, which further prevented him from controlling his business and investments.

Will and Azubah had a son named Henry. To say he didn't get along with his mother was an understatement. One day, after an argument, she cut him out of her will. Henry's eventual cause of death was a cerebral hemorrhage, and his last surviving heir, a daughter named Armenia "Mamie" Hayden, never inherited anything of value and never married. She died in Maine, sick and in debt in 1927. With that, Mercie Dale's curse had come full circle.

It was difficult for successive owners to maintain William Hayden's house in the luxurious style he had intended. Helen Stacy of Albany, Vermont, lived in the house when she was a child. She recalled that her parents, Alfred and Goldie Mason, purchased the place for just $15,000.

In an article on vermonter.com, she was quoted, "My mother saw ghosts [in the Hayden House] at least twice. The first time, she noticed a man sitting in the living room dressed in Lincoln period clothes with a hat similar to what Abraham Lincoln wore. She didn't believe what she was seeing and tried to ignore it. She had a little boy visiting at the time and the boy saw the man too. The child called the spirit 'Pepere,' or 'grandfather' in French, and approached the apparition, which stood up, walked toward the hall and vanished." She continued: "Another time, my mother heard old style ballroom music playing. It seemed to be coming from the dance hall in the upper portion of the house. Sort of like old fashioned waltz music. Curious as to where the music was coming from, she walked to the top of the stairs and the music just stopped."

Helen also said there were a lot of unexplained fires on the property in the nearly three decades she lived there and that they seemed to spring up on their own, like one she saw with her own eyes that began on the roof of an outbuilding with nobody else around.

Through the years, the building fell into a state of disrepair, but it was eventually rescued. Paperwork from the United States Department of the Interior entered January 31, 1978, notes, "In 1957, William Chadwick purchased the house and is currently restoring to its original splendor. To this day, it is said that the house is haunted by the Hayden ancestors."

THAT ROGUE ROYALL TYLER

*H*ave you ever found yourself chatting with a couple at a dinner party and, in making polite conversation, leaned over to ask, "So…where did you two meet?" only to have the gentleman of the two offer, "Oh, we met at the home of her parents! I was twenty, and she was only two"? Creepy as it sounds, Royall Tyler, namesake of the theater at the University of Vermont, could have answered the same.

UVM's nod to Tyler on the campus that was donated by Ira Allen might not have been built if a fire hadn't snuffed out UVM's decrepit gym back in 1886. The students went without a designated physical education facility for more than ten years and were forced to exercise in shacks, which they eventually burned in protest.

Finally, UVM president Matthew Henry Buckham realized that the time had come to rectify this particular campus shortcoming and earmarked $20,000, a decent enough sum in those days, to build a no-frills gym next to the Old Mill. The Old Mill, with its golden dome, serves as an iconic image for the university, sitting on the site of the very first building on campus. To make sure they would end up with a building that would be an aesthetic match for the existing structures on campus, Buckham settled on Boston architectural firm Andrews, Jaques and Rantoul, whose founders were students of renowned architect H.H. Richardson, the man who had designed UVM's Billings Library, with its distinctive arched entry.

I love being inside the Royall Tyler Theater, but when I consider Royall Tyler *the man*, I want to pull a face. Royall Tyler *was* an illustrious playwright

Royall Tyler Theater. *Courtesy the University of Vermont.*

and eminent legal mind, but he was also an opportunistic cad with few social or emotional boundaries who, these days, would likely have been jailed for being a child molester.

I give him props for serving in the Revolutionary War, most notably during Shays' Rebellion, a huge scuffle in Springfield, Massachusetts, in which Daniel Shays led thousands of men in an uprising against economic and civil rights offenses.

In 1787, Tyler wrote *The Contrast.* The first professionally produced play by an American, it satirized European and American culture. Because of his sexual proclivities, he's been featured in a bit of writing, too, by an author whose name might be as familiar or perhaps *more* familiar to you than Royall Tyler's: Nathaniel Hawthorne.

Hawthorne modeled the creepy character Judge Jaffrey Pyncheon from his book *The House of the Seven Gables* after Tyler. It was an idea that came to him in July 1838 thanks to gossip from his wife Sophia's family about Tyler and his abuse of her female relations.

Hawthorne scribed in his notebook: "A political or other satire might be made by describing a show of wax-figures of the prominent public men; and, by the remarks of the showman and the spectators, their characters and public standing might be expressed. And the incident of Judge Tyler as related by E--- might be introduced."

There was plenty of fodder in the relationship between Royall Tyler and Elizabeth to create a scandalous story line, and plenty even before that. Tyler was an arrogant hound dog of a young man who used his intelligence, charm and social stature to worm his way into and out of many a relationship. In 1779, Tyler conceived an illegitimate son named Royal Morse with a cleaning woman named Katharine Morse he'd met at Harvard. He was romantically linked to Abigail Adams, daughter of John Adams (after dallying with her sister), but fouled that up because he wasn't a very attentive suitor.

The story goes that Tyler and Adams fell giddily in love and became engaged, and her parents, believing she could do better, weren't exactly thrilled. On a trip to Europe with her mother, Abigail spent countless hours writing letters to Tyler, but ship after ship sailed in from America without a return response. A heart-to-heart talk with her mother convinced her that her dreamboat was kind of a dud. Abigail dumped Royall Tyler and in 1876 married Colonel William Stephens Smith, a guy her family thought was a much better catch.

Rejected in love, Tyler was heartbroken. Believe it or not, he was living at the time at the home of Abigail's sister, Mrs. Mary Cranch, with whom he'd had a previous relationship. He decided to leave, boarding instead at the home of his friend Joseph Palmer and Palmer's wife, Elizabeth. Still moping over being cast aside, Tyler sought comfort in the arms of his very married landlady.

As for Abigail, I don't think she forgot her affection for Tyler. How could she with her sister Mrs. Cranch rubbing her nose in it? Here's a letter in which she cattily tells Abigail of a blessed event at the Palmer home:

We live in an age of discovery. One of our acquaintance has discover'd that a full grown, fine child may be produc'd in less than five months as well as in nine, provided the mother should meet with a small fright a few hours before its Birth. You may laugh but it is true. The Ladys Husband is so well satisfied of it that he does not seem to have the least suspicion of its being otherways, but how can it be? for he left this part of the country the beginning of september last, and did not return till the Sixth of April, and his wife brought him this fine Girl the first day of the present Month. Now the only difficulty Seems to be, whether it is the product of a year, or twenty weeks. She affirms it is the Latter, but the learned in the obstretick Art Say that it is not possible. The child is perfectly large and Strong. I have seen it my sister: it was better than a week old tis true, but a finer Baby I never Saw. It was the largest she ever had her Mother says. I thought So myself, but I could not say it. It was a matter of So much Speculatın that I was determin'd to see it. I went with trembling Steps, and could not tell whether I should have courage enough to see it till I had Knock'd at the Door. I was ask'd to walk up, by, and was follow'd by her Husband. The Lady was seting by the side of the Bed suckling her Infant and not far from her—with one sliper off, and one foot just step'd into the other. I had not seen him since last May. He look'd, I cannot tell you how. He did not rise from his seat, perhaps he could not. I spoke to him and he answer'd me, but hobble'd off as quick as he could without saying any more to me. There appear'd the most perfect harmony between all three. She was making a cap and observ'd that She had nothing ready to put her child in as she did not expect to want them so Soon. I made no reply—I could not. I make no remarks. Your own mind will furnish you with sufficient matter for Sorrow and joy, and any other sensations, or I am mistaken.

Adieu yours affectionately

Of course, the third person in the room was Tyler, who, it's been said, fathered at least one but possibly *two* daughters with Elizabeth Palmer: Sophia Palmer in 1786 and Catherine Palmer in 1791. When Abigail responded to her sister's letter, she must have been thinking longingly about how dreamy Royall Tyler looked in his fancy scarlet broadcloth coat, white vest, ruffled shirt and knee-length breeches. She took his part in the disgraceful state of affairs, laying the blame at the feet of that cougar, Mrs. Palmer:

In this case it may be difficult to determine which was the Seducer, and I feel more inclined to fix it upon the female than the paramour, at any rate She is more Guilty, in proportion as her obligations to her Husband her children her family & the Religion of which she is a professer are all Scandalized by her and she has sacrificed her Honour her tranquility & her virtue.

You can see how all this is shaping up. Trust me when I say that I haven't even gotten to the creepy part.

Mr. and Mrs. Palmer had a daughter, Mary. As a longtime "family friend," Tyler first met her when she was just a toddler of two and he was a grown man of twenty. Did he remark that he found her clever for her age or that she had remarkable motor skills for a such a little munchkin? No, he did

Abigail Adams Smith. *Courtesy the Library of Congress.*

not. What he did was announce that someday he would *marry* her. He said it again when she was eleven, about the time he took to referring to her as "my little wife."

During his courtship of his future bride, Royall Tyler often called her his "bird in a cage," and I can't help but think there was a whole lot of the kind of grooming going on that had nothing to do with feathers. Writings by Mary's older sister Eliza seem to suggest that no female was safe around Tyler, and it is suspected he molested her while she was growing up too.

Mary, for her part, was thrilled by the attention paid her by the dashing older man. She wrote, years later, in her autobiography, "I certainly loved him…although, it was a purely spiritual love for years." She filled the years just before joining Tyler in holy matrimony by working as a live-in babysitter to her parents' wealthy friends. She also spent time in the home of relatives in eastern New York. It was noticed that she was bright, and as a child she was encouraged to read and write. She even taught school for a period of time.

Royall Tyler married her in secret in 1794, amid speculation she was already pregnant with his child. Together they moved to Guilford and then Brattleboro, Vermont. Mary took time to record the early history of her years in Brattleboro, noting that the women there were all so kind to her because they adored her husband the judge so much. I just bet they did.

It pains me somewhat to say it seems like, when all was said and done, Mary and Royall Tyler were a good match. The judge wrote plays, and Mary ended up writing one of the earliest childcare manuals published by an American woman. She had plenty of material to draw from, since she and her husband had eleven children, and all lived to what in those days would have been considered adulthood. Her book, *The Maternal Physician*, was published anonymously through her husband's printing contacts. It was credited to "AN AMERICAN MATRON" and outlined the new role of child rearing for mothers beyond the customary practices of colonial times.

Mary Palmer Tyler. *Courtesy the University of Vermont.*

Tyler was named professor of jurisprudence at the University of Vermont in 1811, teaching there for several years. In 1812, he made an unsuccessful run for the U.S. Senate. After that, he was made chief justice of the Vermont Supreme Court from 1807 until 1814 and was appointed registrar of probate for Windham County, Vermont, serving until 1822. Finally, with his health declining, he took a breather. In his later years, he wrote three plays, *The Bay Boy*, *The Chestnut Tree* and *Utile Dulci*.

Tyler died on August 16, 1826. The recorded cause was cancer, but an article in the 1833 *Christian Examiner* entitled "Seduction," written by Nathaniel Hawthorne's mother-in-law, Mrs. Elizabeth Peabody, suggests otherwise. With Tyler dead, Mary Palmer Tyler's sister felt free to be candid about the family's unseemly history:

> *We hope we deserve to be called pure, in some good degree; but to us it did not seem to be pure for a polished man of literary eminence, to enter the sanctuary of sleeping innocence, of absolute childhood, for the basest purpose. We did see it, however, and though more than forty years have since passed by, we recollect with almost incredible vividness the shudder of terror and disgust which then shook our infant frame. We have traced the career of that man. He seduced the woman, whose children he would have corrupted, caused the self-murder of a wife and mother, and afterwards married the daughter of that victim. He is dead, and the horrors of his mind, during a lingering disease, were the dreadful fruits of sin; but not of disgrace, for this man had a good standing in society.*

It has been assumed that the "self murder of a wife and mother" refers to another child of Tyler's aborted by Elizabeth, and "the dreadful fruits of sin" refers to venereal disease, since it was widely believed that Tyler's face had wasted away due to syphilis.

A side note regarding Nathaniel Hawthorne: I admire his writing, but not his attitude toward the Irish. Granted, he visited my hometown during a time when the Irish weren't highly regarded (or terribly well behaved), but I object to the priggish way he took it upon himself to look down his nose at Irish men and their children, all while peeking at the cleavage of Irish women. What can you expect from a man who wrote, about Irish elsewhere, that they were "the scum which every wind blows off the Irish shores." Here's what he came up with after visiting Vermont's Queen City in 1836:

Nathaniel Hawthorne. *Courtesy the Library of Congress.*

Nothing struck me more, in Burlington, than the great number of Irish emigrants. They have filled the British provinces to the brim, and still continue to ascend the St. Lawrence, in infinite tribes, overflowing by every outlet into the States. At Burlington, they swarm in huts and mean dwellings near the lake, lounge about the wharves, and elbow the native citizens entirely out of competition in their own line. Every species of mere bodily labor is the prerogative of these Irish. Such is their multitude, in comparison with any possible demand for their services, that it is difficult to conceive how a third part of them should earn even a daily glass of whiskey, which is doubtless their first necessary of life—daily bread being only the second. Some were angling in the lake, but had caught only a few perch, which little fishes, without a miracle, would be nothing among so many. A miracle there certainly must have been, and a daily one, for the subsistence of these wandering hordes. The men exhibit a lazy strength and careless merriment, as if they had fed well hitherto, and meant to feed better hereafter; the women strode about, uncovered in the open air, with far plumper waists and brawnier limbs, as well as bolder faces, than our shy and slender females; and their progeny, which was innumerable, had the reddest and the roundest cheeks of any children in America.

Ah, well. It doesn't pay to be too thin-skinned. After all, Hawthorne is also the guy who wrote *The Scarlet Letter*, one of my favorite books. Maybe I'll read it again, while soaking up some sun on the steps of the Royall Tyler Theater. I can't do anything about Tyler's personal demons, or Hawthorne's, but it seems like a perfect way to exorcise mine.

HOW DRY WE WERE

PROHIBITION IN VERMONT

hinking about Vermont's Prohibition history makes me grin. Maybe it's because these days, the Green Mountain State is practically the beer capital of the United States. Then there's the fact our first constitution, signed in 1777, was drafted in a tavern.

I'm inclined to believe that no one would even try to strip us of our suds these days, as Vermont beer is dear not just to locals but visitors as well. In one documented case, in 2013, an undercover sting resulted in a Vermont attorney being reprimanded for selling a hard-to-find brew, Heady Topper, on Craigslist, and I've known people who reside as far away as North Carolina who've traveled to Vermont to buy cases of craft beer for their own consumption and for friends. I can't say I blame them. Some of our microbrews are so captivating that they've been mentioned in *Bon Appétit* and *Vogue*. Yes, *that* Vogue.

A few years back, I did some tarot readings for a group of women who'd planned a surprise birthday party for a dear friend at a popular Burlington restaurant. The mood was casual, so I had an opportunity to chat with the friend who'd organized the event. While we were discussing business in the Green Mountains, we ended up talking about Vermont's growing craft beer scene. She shared that she was freelancing with a government agency involved in a study about Vermont's burgeoning beer business, a study that might lead to legislation. It seemed that some people in government were worried that more beer being brewed in Vermont would mean more abuse of the beverage. It was a theory I couldn't swallow, but the idea itself came as no surprise. People have been trying to regulate drink here in Vermont since long before the national Prohibition laws of 1920.

There were Vermonters who were vocal about temperance in some form as early as the first decade of the 1800s, but there was little consensus yet on how much or what kind of abstinence was just right. Some people thought that *strong* drink was the issue—that as long as you kept your nose out of the hard stuff, you were doing all right. Others thought that any liquid with an alcohol content—whether hard cider, mead, ale or rum—was the beverage of the devil.

For instance, an 1808 article in the *Green Mountain Patriot* had the headline, "More Beer, Less Rum," a fairly tolerant view. But that same year, a lecturer addressing the Council of Censors of the State of Vermont closed with, "No crime is perhaps attended with more evil consequences to society and individuals than that of drunkenness."

In 1817, there was a big push for temperance in the town of Ryegate, Vermont, whose Scotch-American settlers were said to have carried the penchant for "ardent drink" from their homeland. In their book, *A History of Ryegate, Vermont*, Edward Miller and Frederic Wells noted that early use wasn't much of a problem. Malt and distilled liquors were considered foodstuffs, in everyday use by most settlers, and excused because some thought hard work in the open air caused the ill effects of drink to "dissipate." It was eventually discovered that this wasn't always the case. By the first decade of the 1800s, alcohol was the "bane" of "all the churches in the vicinity." A church elder had built a distillery on his farm, and unfortunately, the church's minister was one of his best customers. Lax attitudes about alcohol gave way to anti-drink sermons on the topic, and not just in places of worship.

In 1828, the Vermont Temperance Society was formed. By the 1830s, many towns were petitioning the legislature to ban all liquor sales, a request that did not go down easy with everyone. As an alternative, licenses were handed out by the county courts, and local citizenry could weigh in on whether a tavern owner or innkeeper's establishment was worthy to obtain one. If you ran a tight ship, with no scandals or public nuisances, you could get a thumbs-up from the community and keep the booze flowing. Complaints could mean the party was over.

Early 1840s temperance supporters in Caledonia County were up in arms over alcohol consumption. There, as in many other corners of Vermont, hard-drinking husbands with an addiction to alcohol were sucking down their wages, leaving their families without two crumbs to rub together. A court weighed in: "Intoxication is prevailing among various individuals in Walden to an alarming extent & the suffering of women & children consequent upon the improper use of spirits by husbands & fathers is but in too many instances extreme."

The mental image of women and children cowering and impoverished because of the habits of a drunken and irresponsible family patriarch was the best advertising tool temperance supporters had at hand. Judges were swayed, as was the heart of the lawmaking machine, Montpelier, where the temperance movement already had plenty of fans. Legislators flirted with the idea of a statewide prohibition and, in 1844, banned the sale of distilled alcohol in all Vermont communities. Always big on municipal control, Montpelier decided to create a "local option" system, making it easy for a community to opt out of the ban. In 1846, they enacted another law, requiring licenses with steep fees for anyone selling distilled liquor, wine or beer. Vermont was drying up, but not fast enough for some people.

Neal Dow. *Courtesy the Library of Congress.*

Enter Neal Dow, mayor of Portland, Maine, and known as the "Napoleon of Temperance." Dow was the son of Quaker parents and an early prohibitionist who had crafted his state's anti-drink laws, which made the use of alcohol for anything but "medicinal, mechanical or manufacturing" purposes illegal. Traveling around the country in 1852 to make his case for what was called the "Maine Law," he visited Vermont and tipped the scales in prohibition's favor. On March 8, 1853, Vermont followed Maine into drink's virtual Death Valley, and prohibition became law.

If you know anything about national Prohibition in the 1920s—or the War on Drugs the United States has been engaged in since 1971—you probably know that plenty of people did not blindly follow these new laws regarding drink as set forth by the state. People could still obtain liquor on the down low, and the treatment of the people engaging in illegal sales was inconsistent, since it was still dependent on the whims of the court and local officials.

A St. Albans woman named Catherine Dillon Driscoll was famous for evading Vermont's temperance laws. An immigrant from Ireland, she was a wily broad with a big personality. Driscoll was in the business of renting out rooms, and her places, with their reputation for free-flowing liquor, were popular among 1840s railroad workers and other men who frequented them. She was arrested over and over but served little time for her scofflaw ways. It was suggested she had an "in" with authorities. Maybe they took the same shine to her she apparently took to some of the railroad men—guys with whom she was *very* familiar.

Driscoll didn't always operate free as a bird. In 1855, she was convicted of twenty-five temperance violations. In a bold move, she sued the sheriff who arrested her, claiming assault, but eventually dropped the charge. Her marital life was also rocky, to say the least. In 1857, she accused her husband, Patrick Dillon, of spousal abuse. His lawyer argued, essentially, that his client's wife was fully capable of beating the bejesus out of him and that Patrick had been the one under *her* thumb—a theory that didn't wash with the judge.

Finally single and fancy free, Catherine was able to amp up her smuggling, boozing ways. In 1860, she was fined again and jailed but broke out, continuing to fill her coffers with the proceeds from her liquor sales. In 1862, police raided her place and seized a huge haul: ten barrels and a keg, with a street value of $1,000. Things then went from bad to worse when a drunken worker named Peter McQuinney died in Driscoll's saloon. She was cleared of wrongdoing when the charges were mysteriously, dropped.

After that, she fell on more hard times when the Messier brothers, Edward and Joseph, assaulted her in an attempted robbery. It's hard to know who got the better of whom in the altercation. Driscoll said that when she saw they came to rob her, she drew a pistol. One of the boys managed to grab her gun, but refusing to be thwarted, she threw a pan of boiling water on the two. They left without the money.

Driscoll's obituary in the *Burlington Free Press*, published on January 11, 1872, seems a pretty soft-pedaled account of her life and time, considering. I have to hand it to the editor for his decorum:

> CATHERINE DRISCOLL DILLON *was a very remarkable woman, and no one had obtained a greater notoriety. She came from Ireland a poor and young woman, with her husband about the time of the building of the Vermont Central and Vermont & Canada railroads in the 1840s. She kept a boarding-house for the laborers along the line of the road, and she*

would relocate her business each season as the railroad construction crews progressed up the Winooski River valley west to Rouses Point on the shore of Lake Champlain.

At her boarding-house whiskey was always available to her boarders and others, in spite of the efforts of the contractors. After the railroads were completed, she moved from Rouses Point to St. Albans, and continued in the same occupation.

About the time the "Maine Law" was first enacted, and for years afterwards, she continued to make life lively for the police forces. Catherine herself, as well as others whom she would hire, brought the contraband to the States. Though difficult to capture, she was arrested scores of times, and as often escaped either from the county jail or from the courts of justice.

Some suspect that Catherine had well-developed relationships with those responsible for enforcing the laws and benefited from their assistance. In 1867 she was indicted by the United States District Court for being connected with smuggling and for trafficking in smuggled liquors. She was convicted and obliged to submit to a fine of $2000 which she paid.

During the time of the Civil War Catherine had become tired of her husband. It is important to remember that Catherine had befriended many railroad workers over the years and perhaps knew every railroad worker by name. She obtained a divorce from her husband, it is claimed, in the following manner:

Mr. and Mrs. Dillon were returning from a trip on the cars when Mr. Dillon failed to find his valise among the baggage on the platform. On Catherine's advice he selected another bag from those in the pile of baggage for the purpose of exchanging the bag for his when his was found. No sooner had they reached home than she procured his arrest for larceny. The unfortunate man was sentenced to Windsor prison, and as a condition of his release, went out in the Vermont Cavalry Regiment as a bugler.

In one way or another Catherine amassed a considerable fortune, variously estimated at fifty to seventy-five thousand dollars. In her younger years she was considered handsome, but later her personal beauty had become somewhat failed, owing to the excessive use of stimulants. At her death she was about forty-five years of age.

In the 1880s, the smuggling continued. A story from the *Burlington Free Press* dated February 3, 1883, and titled "The Rutland Liquor War" indicates that women and men in the southern part of the state were getting their hooch on the quiet, thanks to a Whitehall, New York merchant named O'Neil who owned a wine shop in that city. Patrons would order by mail or telegraph, and their "parcels" would be shipped to them COD by evening rail on what became known as the "jug train." Vermont issued a warrant for O'Neil's arrest with a whopping 457 counts of selling alcohol against the law. Too bad it couldn't be enforced in New York.

By the early 1900s, up north, in Vermont's Queen City of Burlington, there were at least six "whiskey saloons" in the city block of Main Street between St. Paul and South Winooski Avenue. The local option left plenty of wiggle room. Could Vermont ever really be "dry"?

National Prohibition began on January 16, 1920. You might think, by that time, that Vermont would have a handle on temperance, but you'd be wrong. Up in the Northeast Kingdom, smuggling across the border was rampant.

A hygienist in my dentist's office told me a story of how her aunt, a resident of Newport, was a child of seven or eight when, one morning, she arrived at her rural schoolhouse to discover an unsettling scene: the poor teacher was trying to wrangle a handful of children whose trek to school had taken them through a neighbor's field, where they found jugs of whiskey that had been ditched by some spooked smuggler. Curious, they decided to try it and turned up at school drunk as skunks, in no shape whatsoever to learn reading, writing or arithmetic.

Woman's Christian Temperance Union. *Courtesy the University of Vermont.*

Meanwhile, west of Newport, over in Highgate Center, Vermont, alcohol had gone underground, and I mean *way* down under the ground, at the Highgate Manor. The Highgate Manor was built by Dr. Henry Baxter back in the 1860s. He kept his practice there, and it has been widely rumored that the good doctor performed secret medical experiments on the children of the town—and perhaps even on his own children, who didn't live past the age of ten. The house itself was grand, and as it passed out of the hands of the Baxter family, it evolved into a popular vacation destination.

A renovation created a huge dance hall, billed the largest in the North. Benny Goodman and other greats from the big band era visited, making it a favorite nightspot. Visitors loved the inn's amenities and manicured grounds, but most were drawn to its well-appointed underground speakeasy. Mobster Al Capone was one of those. After all, the manor was a short trip from the Canadian border and a perfect place for a kingpin with a hectic bootlegging and prostitution businesses to spend a little quiet time. When authorities asked, while questioning Capone about his involvement in the illegal liquor trade and his Canada connection, he famously answered, "Canada? I don't even know what *street* Canada is on." I've read Capone also made trips from New York to Canada to seek medical attention for his son's hearing issues. A few belts of whiskey after a long day listening to medical specialists was probably just the thing to ease a dad's worried mind.

At regular intervals through the month of January 1920, a warning ran in the *Burlington Free Press*:

Beware boot-leg liquor, warns the United States Public Health Service, for much of it contains wood alcohol and other poisons. An ordinary swallow of wood alcohol may produce death or blindness. Don't risk it.

Vermont certainly wasn't perfect, but local newspapers were filled with more stories of violations of Prohibition laws in New York than right in our own backyard. In October 1920, an incident involving a group of Burlington kids made the news. They found a stash of hidden liquor, ten-quart bottles of Old Crow, behind some buildings on the Flynn Theater block of Main Street. Fortunately, they didn't drink any of the contraband liquor, which was presumed to have come from Canada. Authorities confiscated the batch.

Law or no law, people who were determined could usually always find liquor and feminine companionship. In Burlington in the 1920s,

Al Capone. *Courtesy the Library of Congress.*

with Prohibition in full swing, it was whispered that there was a speakeasy on an upper floor of the old Hotel Vermont. A network of underground tunnels was helpful in moving the booze and broads away from prying eyes. City life had its benefits.

Consider the advantages of some of Vermont's more rural towns, and their possibilities for recreation, especially the "line town" of Richford, Vermont, which sat cheek by jowl with the Canadian border. Presiding over the town's boozy entertainment was a woman named Lillian Minor Shipley, whom the papers liked to call "Queen Lill." Lill was born at Steven's Mills in Richford, in 1886, but left her hometown after marrying a shady character named A.G. Shipley, who was not just a known horse thief but a suspected grave robber too. Maybe he was looking for greener pastures or maybe he thought his luck in Vermont was running out, but whatever the reason, he and Lill took to the road. Going from town to town, they sold patent medicines like celery tonics, which in those days were touted as cure-alls. These unregulated potions could certainly make someone forget their pain for a while, as most were about 20 percent alcohol.

The Shipleys ended up in Boston and Lill opened a brothel, but around 1910, with Beantown cracking down on houses of ill repute, they decided to return to Richford. It was the perfect place for Lill to start plying her old trade. Close to Canada, convenient to the railroad and far from the prying eyes of officials, her business thrived, especially after she built a three-story hotel that literally spanned the border.

While liquor grew scarce elsewhere, Queen Lill could see Canada from her house (pardon my paraphrasing former vice presidential candidate Sarah Palin), which meant a steady supply of firewater. Her place had a big reputation. It was known as the "Palace of Sin," and people wanted in. There were other line houses in the vicinity. You could always find drink at an inn called the Abercorn or take your chances at a shack near the border known as the Bucket of Blood, but if you wanted girls, girls, girls, you had to head to Lill's.

Anti-prohibition propaganda. *Courtesy the Library of Congress.*

The first floor of Lill's had a bar, with upstairs rooms reserved for "private entertainment." The décor was colorful and exotic and populated by accommodating women Lill found in Boston and Montreal. Lill herself was a tough customer. She liked to keep order and was determined to run things her way. She enjoyed her role as a pistol-packing mama and made no secret of what lucrative fun lawbreaking could be. She toured around the town in fancy clothes and an expensive auto. The local police? No problem. She handled them with graft. In 1925, her operation was fined a paltry $150 for trafficking in prostitution, but the smart cookie managed to keep the enterprise afloat through the end of Prohibition's dry spell.

She retired from business and married a farmer named Levi Fleury. During her days as a madam, she invested wisely in land and lived comfortably until her death in 1941.

I don't mean to make it sound like it was all fun and games. Prohibition was a painful and confusing period for many Vermonters, filled with violence, bribery and cultural discrimination. A disproportionate number of Italian and Irish families were targeted for violations. The Irish gained, unfairly, a reputation for escalating the problem of drunkenness and contributing to the demise of society. In 1918, in what was seen as an effort to drive immigrants out, fifteen Caledonia County Italians were prosecuted for liquor violations. Nine got sentences of nine to twelve months plus $400 fines. Sentences were suspended, with warnings not to "furnish or give intoxicating liquor of any kind to any person other than members of [his or her] own family."

While post-Prohibition opinions on the merits and drawbacks of drink still varied wildly, it seemed like alcohol would always be a part of our culture. Vermont grappled with illegal liquor sales even after Prohibition, largely because of the blue laws that kept citizens from purchasing alcohol on Sundays.

On October 15, 1937, Louis Thibault of Windsor pleaded guilty to illegal possession and sale of alcohol, as did Alton C. Howell of Putney, Mrs. Nicolina Pietrodangelo of Rutland and Bernard and Elizabeth Duskie of West Rutland.

In January 1950, attorney Russell Niquette told a group assembled at a State Liquor Board hearing in Barre that there were at least fifteen "speakeasies" in Winooski "between the Eagles Club and the [Winooski] bridge." He was speaking in defense of the Eagles Club. It had a violation for serving an intoxicated man that resulted in a ten-day loss of its liquor license. Niquette argued that the man might have gone to any one of the speakeasies in town before being picked up by police.

In 1954, thirty-nine-year-old Roland Bouchard of Northfield, Vermont, was charged with selling bottled beer and whiskey out of his home *and* his car at double the price of retail stores.

In April 1953, in the city of St. Albans, three men were pulled into court for illegal liquor sales. Webster O. Krupp of the Pontiac Cab Company, Euclide Gadreau and Kenneth Gaboury were raided by state troopers and the Liquor Control Board authorities based on a tip.

In 1961, a huge scandal rocked the city of Burlington when a twenty-four-year-old vice informant named Ed Davies claimed to be engaged in not only illegal liquor sales but also gambling and prostitution. The

Dry no more—M.&F.C. Dorn bottled beer on Pine Street, Burlington. *Courtesy the University of Vermont.*

former welterweight boxer and unemployed father of three told a story of supporting himself while pimping male prostitutes and procuring bottles of hooch for parched folks in the Queen City. His was a saga of dysfunction and bad luck. He was stabbed in a bathroom at the local bus station on St. Paul Street and found bleeding in City Hall Park—retribution, he claimed, for his coming clean to police. He was questioned by authorities for a week about what looked, in those days, like a serious decline in town morals. Two lie detector tests were administered but turned out to be inconclusive. After the stress of it all, he returned to his hometown of Detroit, Michigan, for a break but ended up taking a car that didn't belong to him and driving back to Vermont, where he was charged with interstate car theft. He ended up in the Chittenden County Correctional Center and was eventually sentenced to eighteen months in the federal prison at Danbury, Connecticut.

Even my sainted grandmother was not immune to the lure of making a quick buck selling bootleg booze. Back in 1946, Dorothy O'Leary (I'm her namesake, but so far, no felonious activities have tempted me) was a young mother with five mouths to feed. She lived on Battery Street near Burlington's waterfront. In those days, the waterfront was an eyesore, not the haven for festivals and concerts it is today. It was a neighborhood with a bit of a rough reputation—a place to find cheap housing and regular outdoor games of craps.

Close as it was to Burlington's downtown, you wouldn't have to travel much more than a stone's throw to get liquored up, but Vermont's blue laws meant an absence of alcohol on Sundays. After attending mass, Gram, who was then known as Dot, opened her home to people in the neighborhood who were in need of a little firewater.

When I learned this while searching for other lawbreakers in the archives of the *Burlington Free Press*, I called my mother. "Hey, I have to ask you something. Did Gram have a speakeasy in her house when you were a kid?" She laughed. "Who told you?"

Although she was only five, my mother recalled the situation quite vividly. She told me that her mother was the victim of a sting operation. Normally, Gram, who was the only breadwinner for her brood, would only sell whiskey to people she knew. But one day, a handsome stranger showed up, asking for a belt. Gram had been divorced and single for a while, and it sounds like her hormones got the better of her. When she went for the bottle, her younger sister, whom we all called Do-Do, was skeptical. "Are you really gonna sell it to him?" she asked.

"Why not?" my grandmother answered. "Look at him. He's gorgeous!" Just her luck: her dreamboat was an undercover liquor inspector. In no time there were two more agents bursting through her doors. My mother recalled that she and her older sister had just been Christmas shopping, and she had to stand by and watch them search their packages for the contraband sauce.

Gram made the headlines more than once because of the incident. She pled guilty and, fortunately, was given a suspended sentence. While part of me is shocked that my tiny grandmother was engaged in such activities, another part can't help but be amused. After all, it was a long time ago.

Maybe through the lens of history we can all cast a sober eye on the good and bad aspects of lifting a glass, while hoping that in Vermont, our craft beer cup will always runneth over.

THE DEVIL RIDER

*W*hen I was three, I fell into a snit about something my mother wouldn't let me do. I stomped my little feet (which, during that phase of my life, seemed perennially clad in black patent leather shoes) and threatened to run away from home. How did my mother respond? She went into the bedroom and got a suitcase, put some of my things in it, bundled me into my plaid coat and hat and led me by my pudgy hand to the front porch, where she bid me goodbye and closed the door. It took me only a few minutes to learn my lesson. I howled and begged to be let in. My mother opened the door, took my luggage and ushered me into the house.

It's lucky for her there was no circus in town at the time. I may have been wooed by a ventriloquist and spent a thrilling career under the big top, like Eaton Stone.

Eaton Stone was a Burlington boy, born in 1818 to Davis Stone of Bennington, Vermont, and his wife, Sarah Eaton, of Massachusetts. In 1828, when Eaton was just ten years old, the circus came rolling into Burlington. Here, the facts get a little muddy. Some circus historians point to the troupe being that of Price and Simpson, a group that was merely straggling along after losing most of its animals in a five-day storm while sailing on the ship *Orbit* from Charleston to Baltimore. (According to one account, the animals were lost in the wake of the storm, each engulfed by waves and disappearing over the side of the boat, one after another.)

More likely, the circus belonged to Turner and Howes. "Uncle" Nathan Howes was the older brother of Seth Howes, who was later called the "Father

of the American Circus." He was the first circus owner to bring an elephant to the United States.

Vermont could be a wild place in the early 1800s, but the circus was wilder. An exciting combination of clowns, jugglers, bareback acts, gymnasts, oddities, ventriloquists and a menagerie of trained animals. Unless you lived in a big city, there was little to do for recreation back then, let alone thrills, and the straggling circuses that traveled through Vermont and New England as a whole offered a welcome diversion. The price of a ticket in those days was about a quarter, with children admitted at half price.

How could a young boy resist? During the day, Eaton spent every free moment hanging around the circus and was allowed access to the animals. He was particularly fond of the horses. Eventually, he was befriended by the circus's ventriloquist, who took a shine to the boy, regaling him with tales of the wonders of travel, the excitement of the crowd and the opportunities that could be had for someone with talent. When the circus left Burlington, Eaton left with it.

The situation could have ended with nothing but a lot of misery and hand wringing on the part of Eaton's parents, but as it happened, the Stone family was well off and well connected. Eaton's

Den Stone Circus advertisement. *Courtesy Alabama Department of Archives and History.*

father, Davis Stone, was an attorney and highly regarded in the Burlington community. He filed a suit against the circus and the ventriloquist for kidnapping, and Eaton was returned to Vermont. He didn't stay long. The circus bug had bitten him hard. It wasn't long before he ran away again, this time with a company called Buckley and Weeks.

This time, his father did not pursue him. With Buckley and Weeks, Eaton learned plate spinning and tumbling. He was agile and a quick learner. His real talent, though, was with the horses. Traveling across the United States and into the Southwest, Eaton honed his talent for equine acrobatics. In interviews, he claimed to have been captured by Native Americans and taught their bareback stunts. Those familiar with Stone were apt to believe that most of these stories were fabricated, or at the very least exaggerations. Some writings indicate that it's likely he became friendly with the Indians because of their fascination with his conjuring tricks, learned at the hands of the ventriloquist his father sued. However it happened, his act grew increasingly western and flamboyant. "Tribeswomen," he said, had created his beaded buckskin outfits. It was great PR. His billing changed from the "Monkey Rider" to "Devil Rider."

Nobody could dispute Stone's talent on the back of a horse. Hurtling along at astonishing speeds on a seemingly wild animal, he performed stunts that amazed and terrified audiences. He could do a somersault on the back of a lightning-fast stallion, jump to the ground and swing back up with dazzling speed. Sometimes he'd lead the horse in a vault over the ring and into the stands, eliciting shrieks from the audience. He entertained crowds all over the continent and in Europe. He was, quite possibly, the most famous bareback performer of his day.

He was once quoted in an interview as saying, "From early childhood I liked horses, and took to riding as naturally I suppose as young ducks do to water. I commenced in the ring at eight years of age [historical articles indicate this was an exaggeration] and enjoyed riding so much that there never was any paying necessary to make me work, and nothing could have induced me to leave off."

Eaton wasn't the only Stone to make headlines in the circus world. To add insult to injury, his brother, Den Stone, named after a well-known Vermont judge, ran off to join the circus, too, working first as a popular clown and later as the owner of his own traveling company.

Dennison W. Stone was born in 1824, six years after his famous brother. He began his circus career with Ira Coles, a descendant of William H. Cole, a renowned contortionist. His career as a clown blossomed (I hope with

The Amateur Circus. *Courtesy the Library of Congress.*

a squirting flower) in 1840, thanks to a reportedly hysterical pantomime of the story of Mother Goose. Two years later, he was on track for circus management. The list of companies he presided over is long: Stone & McCollum, Stone & Madigan, Stone & Murray, Den Stone's Circus, Central Park Menagerie and, by 1878, Stone's Grand Circus and Musical Brigade. Greasepaint may have been in his blood, or maybe it was just a love of applause. He continued to clown through most of his career. That and being a hometown boy would play to his advantage during Vermont's circus ban.

To public officials in the mid-1800s, circuses meant high spirits, high spirits led to carousing and carousing to strong drink. Enter Stone, Rosston & Murray, whose part-owner was not just a clown of some renown but also the son of one Vermont judge (and named after another). Stone sent advance word by way of friends and relatives in the Green Mountain State, and when bills were posted announcing their intended performances, nobody put up a fuss. They modified their act, removing the equestrian aspect. For each performance, Rosston would respectfully declare to those assembled that while they were there to entertain, they had no desire to break the law by "putting on a circus." Then he would announce that they *did* happen to have horses and riders with them, should the audience care to see them. A rider and horse would already be peeking from behind the curtain, ready to whet the crowd's appetites. Then, out would come Den Stone and what was billed as his "Inexhaustible Budget of Fun" shouting his welcome. The audience would go wild, calling for them to bring out the horses and riders, often chanting "Den Stone! Den Stone!"

It was a clever gambit, and Stone, Rosston & Murray traveled the state to decent financial success. The book *Olympians of the Sawdust Circle* by William L. Slout noted that on a later tour through Vermont in 1865, billed as "Den Stone's Circus and Central Park Menagerie," Stone cleared $30,000, helping to pave the way to a secure old age.

After the Civil War, Stone's company was the first to appear in many southern cities. He was the first circus manager, it's been recorded, to travel from point to point by boat and rail.

His last adventure under the big top was in 1878, a last-ditch effort to bring a high-class one-ring circus back to life. Den Stone died in Franklin, New Jersey, on April 20, 1892. He had given the circus fifty-four years of his life. He was sixty-eight.

As for Eaton Stone, he retired after forty years in show business, having accumulated a small fortune. He owned more than two thousand acres of property around the country but eventually settled in Nutley, New Jersey, where he bought a large farm with fruit trees. He rented rooms and boarded horses. A brownstone quarry was discovered on his land, which further increased his wealth.

In 1894, after twenty-seven years of retirement, the seventy-six-year-old "Devil Rider" was approached by Henry C. Bunner, a Nutley resident and also editor of *Puck* magazine. It was Bunner's plan that the town use Stone's farm and six-sided practice barn to create an amateur circus and sell tickets, with proceeds to found a local chapter of the Red Cross.

Stone threw himself into the project, not only loaning his barn and grounds but also training the acts. A March 25, 1894 article in the *New York Times* reported that the event was sold out and was standing room only. Legendary sharpshooter Annie Oakley was one of the performers. She shot glass balls out of the air while riding backward on her horse, borrowed for the festivities by a local delivery company. Then it was Stone's turn. He

Young Annie Oakley. *Courtesy the Library of Congress.*

was the highlight of the evening. The septuagenarian rode bareback into the ring, set his horse to galloping, stood fully upright and then crouched. The crowd gasped and then cheered, delighted, as he spread his arms wide, turning a perfect backflip. Eaton Stone died in Nutley, New Jersey, on August 8, 1903.

THE MURDER OF SALLY GRISWOLD

*S*arah Walker Griswold was a risk taker and an adventurer. If not for that fact, she might never have enjoyed the comfortable life she once had in Vermont or owned the stately Federal-style house that still stands in the town of Williston. But then she might also never have been murdered.

In 1849, Sally and Ephraim Griswold were farmers struggling to make ends meet when they began to hear a growing hubbub about get-rich-quick opportunities offered by the California Gold Rush. Scraping together whatever means they could, they went west to find their fortune. Instead of improving their lot, they fell on more hard times, and Ephraim, feeling like life in California wasn't panning out for him, returned home to Vermont. Sally decided to stay, and it turned out to be a smart move. There was wealth to be found on the perimeter of the gold rush, and Sally knew it. She opened a boardinghouse, charging exorbitant prices for little extras like food. She became part of a Sacramento Vigilance movement, a group of prominent citizens and business owners with a vested interest in driving the corrupt politicians and an ever-growing unsavory element out of town.

When Sally did come back to Vermont, her pockets weren't empty. The woman had saved more than $10,000, a fortune in those days—enough capital to do just about anything she wanted. What she wanted was a home that would be the envy of all who knew her, so she built a two-story brick house on St. George Road, a homestead with 140 acres of land. The house

Juniper Hill Farm, Sally Griswold's dream home, January 1960. *Courtesy Walter A. Stultz.*

was luxuriously appointed and had a view of Lake Champlain. She called the place Juniper Hill Farm.

Sally was more than comfortable. She was content. Her husband, a guy without a lot of motivation or self-discipline, was still around, but Sally was unquestionably the head of the Griswold household. Her smart West Coast business dealings meant she and Ephraim had everything they could want, and everybody knew it. That became a problem when their foster daughter, Adelia, married a n'er-do-well named Charles Potter.

Adelia was born the daughter of Sally's sister. She and Ephraim had taken her into their care when she was just three weeks old. Sally adored the girl and took her responsibilities as a mother seriously. She was concerned about Adelia's relationship with Potter from the get-go. Try as she might to like him, she couldn't get over the feeling that he was no good. Her instincts would prove correct.

As years passed, Sally became more independent from Ephraim. She slept in a parlor off the kitchen and ran the farm herself with no in-house servants aside from a houseboy, a child of twelve named Edward Call.

In 1862, Adelia and Charles needed a place to stay. Charles, who had been running a tavern across the Canadian border, spent money like it was water. Sally knew this, but for Adelia's sake, she took them in anyway. It was an unfortunate arrangement. Potter continued his spendthrift ways, and Sally wasn't silent about what she thought of it. They argued about petty things; for instance, when they moved in, Potter made a big deal about the need to install new locks, but Sally didn't want to make a hole in the door. Their arguments drifted over to Adelia. Soon she and Sally began to snipe at each other, too. It was Sally's custom to rise in the morning and prepare the family breakfast. After a time, Adelia prickled at that, perhaps hoping for a little domesticity of her own. Some of their tensions ran so hot that they erupted in physical violence. The couple finally moved a short distance away, but absence did not make hearts grow fonder.

Years passed and Potter still resented the woman, who always seemed to be up in his business. He and Adelia began trying to convince Sally, no longer a young woman, to turn the farm over to them. When she resisted, they tried to have her committed. Finally, after many a rocky domestic episode, it looked like something had to give. Potter took a trip by train to New York City. There, he found a gangster willing to travel to Vermont to take care of Sally, once and for all. His name was John Ward (aka Jerome Lavigne). His price was $500 plus whatever valuables he managed to find in the house. Returning to Williston, Potter arranged a trip to Canada with his wife, their two children, his brother *and* his wife's adopted father. It was generally thought at the time that Ephraim Griswold, who claimed in court he'd been planning to make the trip to Canada anyway, had given his tacit approval to the scheme.

Ward traveled by train to Vermont, and he'd already met with Potter at a hotel in Essex to finalize the plan. According to Ward, the two agreed that Potter would file the door latch to make entering the home easier. On the morning of August 27, 1865, the travelers left for Canada, and the plan began to unspool.

John Ward made his way to Juniper Hill Farm. Waiting for dark, he planned his attack, thinking he'd have no problem murdering Sally Griswold in her sleep.

To his surprise, when he broke into the house, his intended victim was not in bed but in the kitchen. His original plan foiled, he rushed toward Sally, striking her in the head with a blackjack and stabbing her several times. Once she was unconscious, he turned his attention to Edward, the houseboy. Wanting to make sure he could not escape his sleeping quarters, Ward locked the door from the outside. Then he returned to the house to finish his work with Sally. He sliced her throat from ear to ear and then ransacked the place. Finally, he wrapped Sally's body and carried it from the house.

Stairs in the ell that led to Edward Call's sleeping quarters, 1960. *Courtesy Walter A. Stultz.*

In the morning, at about seven o'clock, a man named Morris Sullivan came calling. A neighbor of the Griswolds', he'd arranged the day before to borrow their wagon and had arrived bright and early to get it. What he got instead was a sorry state of affairs. The boy, locked up in his loft, was screaming frantically to be let out. There was blood on the doorstep of the house, and inside, furniture was upturned as though there had been a terrible struggle. After some searching by authorities, Sally was found in a calf pen near her barn, wrapped in a bloody blanket.

Sally Griswold was a small woman, about five feet tall and 130 pounds, but everyone who knew her considered her "feisty." Postmortem reports acknowledged that she fought hard against her assailant. Her arms and legs were bruised. Her skull was fractured, and her face and neck had been stabbed numerous times, including a gash that drew a line from her lip to just under her chin and a slice to the jugular that finally, mercifully, ended her life.

The community was up in arms over the murder, and a special detective was hired to get to the bottom of the heinous crime. Before long, it was discovered that a conductor on a southbound train had noticed a man riding on his route who fit Ward's description and looked very suspicious indeed. Although it was August, he had boarded the train wearing a heavy overcoat, which he declined to remove, something the conductor found peculiar. Unfortunately for Ward, the coat wasn't long enough to cover his shoes, which the train employee noticed were spattered with blood. The railroad notified law enforcement, and an alert was posted.

It's entirely possible that we're not discussing the brightest light on the porch where committing a criminal act is concerned, as a week later, impatient for his cash, Ward traveled north, again by train. Once he had gotten his payoff, he headed home, never suspecting he had company. Detective Noble B. Flannagan had tailed him. Ward was apprehended, and he and Potter were both charged with the murder of Sally Griswold.

The trial for the murder of Sally Griswold began on April 9, 1866, and it was all people talked about. The *Burlington Free Press* ran special promotions in its papers promising complete coverage.

After a week of grueling testimony, the court found Potter innocent of his charges but declared Ward guilty and sentenced him to death by hanging. Not everyone agreed on the verdict. The *Free Press*, in an editorial, noted, "The community cannot be persuaded, probably, that Ward was anything more than an agent of an abler and more guilty instigator." During the trial, it was noted that the perpetrator seemed to be, for a stranger, "tolerably familiar" with the layout of the house. People shook their heads trying to wrap their brains around how just one person had managed to overcome so handily both the feisty woman and the teenaged houseboy.

While Ward sat in the hoosegow, awaiting execution, he tried, unsuccessfully, to convince New York cronies, and even Potter, to help him make a break for it. Potter, as you can imagine, declined.

John Ward was executed at the State Prison in Windsor on March 20, 1868, but not before making a detailed confession. In it he suggested he was not alone on the night of the murder. Despite the baring of his soul, Ward was sent off to meet his maker. Papers described the scene. The gallows were black, with a platform nine feet long by seven feet wide, standing five feet above the pavement. The seven-foot beam rose over two trapdoors, although only one was needed. The noose that ran through the beam and around the criminal's neck was attached to a spring, which would give a stronger jerk of the neck than simply rope alone, as the body fell through the opening created by the trapdoor.

On the scaffold, hands tied, Ward was heard to sigh several times as the constable adjusted the noose around his neck. He had one last thing to say to the fifty-odd witnesses assembled: "Now, as I am to appear before God, I humbly state what is true. I neither struck nor injured the old lady. Her blood is not on my hands, although I knew and in fact participated in the murder. If that constitutes murder, then I am a murderer"

The *Burlington Free Press* recorded what happened next: "The cap was drawn over his eyes, and Sheriff Stimson said, 'The time has now arrived when the extreme penalty of the law must be executed upon you, John Ward, alias Jerome Lavigne. God have mercy on your soul.' The next instant the trap was sprung, and the murderer of Mrs. Griswold was launched into eternity." I'm thinking the line should have read "accused murderer," and I'm mad as a hornet there wasn't another perp, or a few more, hanging on the gallows that day.

Plenty of people believed Ward's version of the story, especially since not long after he was hanged, a crime with some very familiar culprits was committed at Smith Wright's store in Williston. The case of the *State vs. Charles H. Potter and Hamilton Potter* outlines a complaint of burglary and a discovery of the goods at the home of the Potters and Ephraim Griswold. It's enough to make anyone in their right mind think twice about who was guilty and who was innocent in the murder of Mrs. Griswold.

On June 15, 1868, Smith Wright arrived at his general store at the corner of Oak Hill and Williston Roads to find broken glass, blood on the floor and pry marks on a back window.

A quick check revealed about $1,000 in merchandise missing from the premises. Outside, Wright found clear wagon tracks he suspected belonged to the thieves. He contacted Sheriff Noble Flanagan, and the two men followed the trail to the Griswolds' property, where they immediately found a wagon. They measured it to make sure the width corresponded to the tracks they had followed. Flanagan had a hunch the goods were there, so he stationed men in the area to watch the house. On Tuesday morning, he headed back to Juniper Hill. Adelia was home, as were her two children, Charles and Katie, plus a lame boy presumed to be a hired hand, as well as a hired girl.

Flanagan told Adelia that he had a warrant to search the premises, so she let him in, but he found nothing. He went back to town, and while eating his breakfast, he recalled something. The Potters had a hired man named

Stephen Foster. He hadn't seen him at the house, so where was he? Flanagan soon learned that he had ridden off with a neighbor, Mr. Walker, and he immediately sent men out to find him. Meanwhile, Smith Wright had given him a list of some of the merchandise he was missing. Now that he knew what he was looking for, he went back with Wright to search the house again.

This time, he found what he was looking for. The skeleton keys were in a pile of rubbish near an outbuilding. The stolen items were tucked away in Ephraim's room, behind the bed and under the rug. Flanagan discovered a hole in the floorboards about two by three feet wide and at least four feet deep. It was crammed to the top with the stolen items. (In court, Ephraim was questioned about the hole and said his son-in-law had cut it in order to hide liquor, and there were some partial casks of whiskey recovered.)

Foster was not found at the Walkers', but he was found, picked up in Canada on a charge of passing counterfeit money and for the burglary in Williston. He ended up singing like a bird, possibly because the authorities from Vermont played him like a fiddle.

Charles Potter; his brother Hamilton, who was a doctor from New Jersey; and Adelia had been arrested and were being held in jail, while the law leaned hard on Foster, claiming that they had evidence to indicate he had committed the burglary at Smith Wright's place all by himself.

Foster was not about to take the blame for this little drama alone, especially since his was only a part. He told them what he knew, that he had known Charles Potter for years, had met him in Canada and had only been living with the Potters at Juniper Hill since early May. He worked the farm, making one dollar a day, but he had money troubles and it wasn't enough. One evening, during a conversation with Potter, Foster mentioned that life would be a lot easier if he could come up with $250. Potter didn't ask about the sum but suggested they could make the money easily if they hit Smith Wright's general store, adding they would have to wait until more merchandise was delivered.

Foster told authorities that the next time the topic arose, it was Adelia who brought it up, saying it would be "a very easy matter" to get the goods from Smith Wright's. Charles agreed, but later, during a different conversation, they talked about a different place they could hit, a woolen mill, that would be twice as lucrative. The only problem was that it was farther away. During yet another conversation, Potter was back to talking about Smith Wright's, bragging that he could get some keys forged that would fit the door. He told Foster it would be no problem to hide the goods in the house. He said he'd hidden things before, and the places were never discovered. Keys and a hiding place—it was the beginning of a plan. Potter was laying the groundwork, but Foster would carry the scheme out with none other than Adelia.

Once the keys were secured, Adelia took Foster aside, explaining that Charles was a little "skittish" at doing the burglary but assuring him that *she* was not afraid to go. At midday on the fourteenth, it was Adelia who instructed Foster how to load the wagon. It was Adelia who decided which horse would pull it. She went over with him how, once they gained access to the store, he must choose only the finest, most expensive items. She got into the wagon wearing a plain calico dress, a man's brimmed wool hat pulled low over her head, and they set off.

They got to the store at about midnight. Foster attempted to open the door with the keys Potter had given him, but they weren't a match. Adelia, with a chisel from the wagon, helped him pry open the window. He entered the building and gathered up the items, passing them to Adelia, who stood watch outside.

On July 15, 1868, the *New York Times* published this article about the court proceedings:

TRIAL FOR ROBBERY IN VERMONT
Burlington, Vt., Tuesday, July 14

The examination before the Grand Jury of the Potter family, for robbery of Smith & Wright's [sic] store, at Williston, Vt., took place to-day. Stephen Foster, one of the burglars, turned State's evidence. He says he and Mrs. Potter committed the robbery. Her husband, Charles Potter, had gone to Canada for the purpose of getting Dr. Hamilton J. Potter, of Trenton, N.J. away from the scene. Dr. Potter was released. Charles Potter and wife were bound over in the sum of $5,000 each for trial in September.

The case went to trial as planned. Public interest was intense, for obvious reasons. Here was a couple who had just been at the center of a murder trial and was now up on charges of burglary, accessory to burglary and possession of stolen property. There were some, inside and outside the courtroom, who questioned whether Charles Potter was culpable. Yes, he'd gotten the keys, but he was out of the country, so how did he commit the crime? There was also a point brought up that he had been duped by Foster; after all, he had made the keys for Foster's use. It was a question for the jury to decide "whether he is such a man as to be easily imposed on in this way." It's a question for me, too. Because an interesting point in Adelia's defense was whether or not *she* could be charged with the crime at all, since the law presumed back then she couldn't possibly have free will in such an incident and stated that "a woman is presumed to be acting under the influence of her husband." Even more interestingly, she's the one who brought that little tidbit up in court.

On October 3, 1868, a jury found the pair guilty on charges of having "tools adapted and designed with the intention to commit burglary." The decision was appealed and heard by the Vermont Supreme Court the following January.

State v. Potter, 42 Vt. 495, 499 (Vt. 1869), includes this finding: "Adelia's connection with the transaction was during the absence of her husband, when she was free from his immediate influence and control, and if the jury found that she had the keys in her possession, and was carrying out their common intent, as before stated, she was then legally responsible."

Delia and Charles were sentenced to seven years in prison. The "Births" section of the *Burlington Free Press* indicates that while incarcerated, in May 1870, Adelia gave birth to a daughter. The child lived only three months. She is buried next to her mother, who died two years later from an infection caused by an injury she had suffered during a jail brawl. Charles died in 1882. All three are buried at Eldridge Cemetery in South Burlington, Vermont.

I'm convinced that the mastermind of the Smith Wright's burglary was Adelia. If that's true, isn't it just as likely that Adelia was the architect of her own adopted mother's murder? She had the motive, the nerve and a lackey of a husband who possessed the criminal contacts to get the job done. Unfortunately, in her greed, one misdeed fell too quickly on the heels of the other, proving that there was something critical she did not have: a sense of timing.

THE HERMIT OF CHAMPLAIN

*I*t would be hard to drive down Burlington's Battery Street without noticing the beautiful Greek Revival mansion that houses the Pomerleau Real Estate company. It was built for railroad magnate Timothy Follett, whose life was a bit of a rags-to-riches story. He used to be my hero. Now I'm not so sure.

Follett was born in Bennington, Vermont, and transplanted to Burlington as a young boy after his father, a silversmith, passed away. The ambitious man became a lawyer, but it would be a mistake to think that law was all he was interested in. A "Type A" personality, Follett was a big thinker and multitasker who knew how to seize an opportunity.

With two partners, he built the warehouse and wholesale outlet on Burlington's waterfront that today we call the Old Stone Store. The place was the heart of their business dealings on the wharf back when Battery Street was called Water Street and was known as the main commercial hub of the city.

Timothy Follett was the first president of the very first Merchants Bank in the state of Vermont, and he was a driving force behind the Rutland and Burlington Railroad Line. He became the first president of that, too. The idea of the railroad line consumed Follett—when there was a missing piece Follett needed in order to connect it to the Vermont Central Railroad line to make his vision complete, he didn't take it lightly. It was a piece of land—water rights, really—behind a building on Burlington's waterfront owned by Isaac Nye.

Isaac Nye was a businessman who had arrived in Burlington with his parents as a small child. He owned many properties, including a store on the edge of Courthouse Square, now occupied by Burlington's City Hall Park. His lakefront property was the building that today houses the popular Burlington seafood restaurant Shanty on the Shore, situated on a plot of land originally part of a parcel owned by Revolutionary War figure Ira Allen. Allen sold the land to Captain Stephen Keys, who had the first retail store on the site in 1797. After that, the property passed to Gideon King, whose family were some of the original landholders in the city.

It was King who sold the land to Nye at a price just under $900. Nye built his house and store on the site in 1833, and when he did, he built it to last. An article in the *Burlington Free Press* dated October 31, 1990, credits Nye and the building's heavy timber construction (along with its modern sprinkler system) for saving the building from serious damage during a fire that occurred the day before.

The location is layered with historic significance. The second passenger steamboat in the world was built under an oak tree on the same site. It was the steamboat *Vermont*, the first to operate on Lake Champlain in 1809. It was built by a man named Samuel Morey. Forget what you learned in school about Robert Fulton being the guy who invented the steamboat. Morey and a man named John Fitch had earlier patents, but history is a funny thing. Neither Fitch nor Morey got the glory.

Nye was a commissioner in the city, and he was no slouch at business. He built his wharf on what is now King Street. Back then, it was called "Nye's Dock" and "Nye's Wharf." These days, it's the "King Street Ferry Dock," with the honor going to Gideon King. As my husband said when I pondered the reason why, "'Smuggler' trumps 'hermit.'"

Nye was well respected in business, but his reputation as a straight-up guy didn't stop people from talking about him behind his back. Townspeople had no clue what to make of this man who didn't drink, smoke, gamble or chase women; he also had a really weird hobby. Isaac Nye liked to attend funerals. He didn't have to know the deceased. Many times, he didn't. But that didn't stop him from making sure his was the last wagon in the procession to the graveyard. Once there, he would wait until everyone paid their respects and the coffin was covered, and then he'd turn and head for home.

In his store, he rarely spoke unless spoken to. He took his meals, prepared by the wife of a family who rented the upper story of his home, with James Fogarty, an Irish orphan he'd taken in.

The Shanty on the Shore, site of Nye's store. *Courtesy Roger Lewis.*

In 1850, along came Timothy Follett, offering money for the water rights behind his store. Nye said no. Follett wasn't happy. He needed those rights. He made his case to the Vermont Supreme Court, a body with which he was well familiar. A commission was appointed to decide on a fair price for the property.

The figure they came up with was $1,700. Isaac Nye said no to that too, and in 1851, he appealed the decision. Pending the appeal, the railroad was supposed to deposit $1,700 into a bank account in his name. It was assumed that they did as they were told, tucking it safely away in the Merchants Bank, across from Nye's store, the bank Timothy Follett created. The name of the bank had come from another business Timothy Follett owned: the Merchants Lake Boat Line.

The lawyers battled it out, and the case went on and on. Some people thought that Nye was holding out because he wanted more money than the railroad was offering. Others thought it was just that Nye was such a peculiar person. Of course, he was in no hurry to settle the case. He was never in a hurry to do anything.

While all this was going on, Isaac Nye wrote to his brother, who lived in Champlain, New York. He said that business was now distasteful to him, and rather than be troubled by that, or what he called "the law's delays," he closed his store and retreated further from society.

In the early days, after he abandoned his business, people would arrive and be surprised to find a locked door, and some thought he'd change his mind. But they soon realized that Nye wasn't fooling around. There was plenty of gossip around town about the wastefulness of it all. Not just the goods, still in the store, but also Nye's "raft of spars," a collection of expensive masts that were lashed together and floating, tied to a mooring behind the house. This he let the children of the neighborhood use as a floating dock. Over time, the masts rotted and were of no use to anyone.

Timothy Follett. *Courtesy Thea Lewis.*

In 1870, Isaac Nye died at home. His request, true to his quirky style, was that he be laid on the counter where he had done business in the old days so people might pay their respects. Nothing was cleaned, mind you. There were cobwebs everywhere, and the goods he had once intended for sale had "mouldered on the shelves." There was still no resolution of the court case.

His two brothers were his executors and heirs, and one of them died with the case still undetermined. From time to time, a commissioner would die, too, and have to be replaced with a new one, who would have to get up to speed. The legal wrangling dragged on.

Finally, in 1878, twenty-seven years after all the contentiousness began, Nye's last named heir and the commission thought they were about to reach a conclusion. Timothy Follett was dead, having passed away four years before Nye after being fired from his position with the Rutland and Burlington. Financially overextended and mired in questionable business dealings, he had gone bankrupt. He was unable to take care of himself due to illness and a diminished mental capacity, so a guardian was appointed to handle his affairs. In the last year of his life, the guardian helped liquidate his assets to satisfy the bank, buying up many of Follett's properties for himself at a fraction of their original worth. Timothy Follett died penniless and alone in a local sanitarium. The final blow? His stately home, designed by architect Ammi Young, who also designed the Treasury Building in Washington, D.C., was purchased in bankruptcy by his rival, Henry Campbell, the president of the Central Vermont Railway.

The Follett House.
Courtesy Roger Lewis.

In 1878, Nye's brother said, essentially, "Enough is enough" about the $1,700 and the long, meandering work of the commission, expressing the desire to get the case settled once and for all. That's when it was revealed by the court that there was no sign of the money Timothy Follett's bank was supposed to be holding in trust for Isaac Nye; $1,000 in damages was awarded to Nye's remaining heir, but nobody could figure out exactly how the railroad company, which still owned the land but was bankrupt, could be forced to pay after all the water that had gone under the bridge—or, in this case, under filled land. It was suggested that maybe the bank should cough up the funds. The point was pondered, but in the end, nobody got paid.

The *Burlington Free Press* cleverly weighed in that if Charles Dickens, who had been a young man when Nye's case against the railroad began, had its facts and characters, "he would have had material for a novel which might have rivaled, Bleak House."

The *Burlington Free Press* reported on October 23, 1857:

> *Death of Hon. Timothy Follett.—The Hon. Timothy Follett, for many years a leading businessman of Burlington, and a prominent politician, died in this place, on Monday evening of last week. To him, probably more than to any other man, is Vermont indebted for the construction of the Rutland and Vermont R.R., and to his connection with this enterprise is mainly attributed the loss of a large fortune, which so weighed upon his mind, as gradually to prostrate his intellect and physical powers, and sink to him to [the] helplessness of a child. Mr. Follett was a public-spirited man, and aided greatly in making Burlington the largest and most prosperous commercial town in Vermont. His age was about 66 [sic] years.*

BORN OVER THE BORDER

*W*hen you think of a "birther movement," you probably picture a United States president who was lampooned for his oversized ears. It may surprise you to learn that the first famous birther controversy swirled not around President Barack Obama but rather a different commander in chief, a guy whose massive muttonchop sideburns would be at home in any barbershop quartet. Can you name the president with a display of fuzz so fantastic it routinely takes the top spot on lists that include the facial hair of Harrison, Van Buren and Lincoln? The answer is Chester Arthur.

Chester A. Arthur became the nation's "21" back in 1881 upon the assassination of President James A. Garfield. He's been called "America's most obscure President," and it's true that until the hue and cry for President Obama's birth certificate, few people I knew could scrabble up many facts about him. It's likely the circumstances of his birth would have held no intrigue for anyone but his immediate family if President Garfield hadn't died unexpectedly and upset the constitutional apple cart.

By most accounts, Chester A. Arthur arrived on October 5, 1829, the fifth child of Malvina (Stone) and William Arthur, who met while teaching at the same school in Dunham, Quebec. Malvina was born in Berkshire, a town in Franklin County, Vermont. (It's a region famous for farms, maple syrup festivals and illegal liquor trade during Prohibition.) Sometime after her birth, her parents immigrated to Canada, where she eventually met William, who was born in Cullybackey, Ireland, but had come most recently from Dublin.

Chester Arthur House, Schenectady, New York—later the Jersey Ice Cream Factory. *Courtesy Grems-Doolittle Photo Collection.*

William became a traveling preacher, moving back and forth across a border that was much more open than the one we know today. At the time he and Malvina were expanding their family, childbirth could be a scary proposition since infant and mother mortality rates were much higher than they are today. In the first part of the 1800s, babies were born at home, often without aid of a doctor, because doctors were scarce. At the time of Chester's birth, his grandparents were living in Bedford, Quebec. It's been wondered: with her husband traveling, did Malvina seek the security of her parents' home at this critical time, not just for herself and the baby but for her older children, too?

As he grew up, nothing about Chester Arthur seemed very mysterious. He was, for a time, a schoolteacher, a profession he began while still a teenager. But after attending Union College in Schenectady, New York, he studied law in Ballston Spa and eventually began practicing in New York City. He won several high-profile civil rights cases, including *Jennings v. Third Avenue Railroad*, a victory for Elizabeth Jennings Graham, a black woman denied a seat on a Manhattan streetcar. The case led to the desegregation of the streetcar system. Arthur was just twenty-four at the time.

He joined the Republican Party, and in the late 1850s, he became a member of the New York State Militia. During the Civil War, as quartermaster general for the State of New York, he organized food and supplies for Union soldiers. After the war, thanks to the finagling of friend and political boss Roscoe Conkling, he was named customs collector for the Port of New York.

As customs collector, Arthur controlled about one thousand jobs and threw plenty of them to Conkling's supporters, who, in turn, contributed to the Republican Party. This shadiness was foiled when Rutherford Hayes became president and tossed Arthur from his job. Arthur went back to practicing law but remained a staunch supporter of Republican ideals.

I love playing the party game "If you could have dinner with anyone, dead or alive, who would it be?" In this case, I don't even need dinner. I don't need a one-on-one with anyone. I'd settle for video of the 1880 Republican National Convention, to see the political maneuvering that took place that day.

The Republicans couldn't decide on their nominee, and Chester Arthur's old friend Conkling, as leader of the stalwart Republicans, was heading up the charge to give Ulysses S. Grant a third term. But the moderate reformist faction of the party, called the "Half-Breed" Republicans, wanted Senator James Gillespie Blaine. Blaine, a former newspaper editor from Maine and early supporter of President Lincoln, knew his way around a podium, and the "Half-Breeds" liked his style. There was a deadlock that lasted until the thirty-sixth ballot, when James A. Garfield, a nine-term senator from Ohio, was unexpectedly nominated. To make sure it would be a done deal, Conkling's lieutenants, acting without his knowledge, advanced Arthur's name as VP to balance the ticket. Bingo! Plays like that are the reason politics is one of my favorite spectator sports.

Like modern-day birthers did over Barack Obama's origins, 1880s Democrats lost their minds over Arthur's nomination. Pointing out that he was likely not even a U.S. citizen, they hired New York lawyer Arthur P. Hinman to investigate the candidate's humble beginnings. Hinman, who eventually wrote *How a Subject of the British Empire Became President of the United States*, originally argued the half-baked theory that Arthur was born in Ireland and didn't come to the United States until he was fourteen, but the story was easily debunked. More enlightening is Hinman's journey to Canada, where he chatted up acquaintances of Malvina's parents, who made no bones about the story they took as fact—Arthur had been born in the country innocently enough, by accident, while his mother was on a visit.

The Honorable Roscoe Conkling. *Courtesy the Library of Congress.*

Now, Canada is a lovely land. Some of my favorite comedians and one of my favorite bands, the Barenaked Ladies, hail from the Great White North. As I write this, Justin Trudeau is the country's prime minister. (Did you just feel your eyes light up?) But while I love Canada, and while people who aren't too knowledgeable about geography mistake Vermont for Canadian territory all the time, you couldn't, in 1829, be born to an Irish father and a mother who had no right to confer her citizenship (that wouldn't happen until the 1930s) and grow up to be president of the United States of America.

Good thing for Chester Arthur the controversy didn't gain much traction. One thing that helped was that while he'd previously just about been the poster child for cronyism, he denounced patronage and became a vocal proponent of merit-based government appointments.

He campaigned actively, devising strategies and coordinating meetings in the Midwest. Some think he may have been the first advance man in American politics. The Republican ticket beat the Democrats in the popular vote by less than one-tenth of 1 percent, but the Electoral College was a different story. Garfield and Arthur won 214 to 155.

How did the future VP celebrate? He went on a $700 shopping spree at Brooks Brothers. Now, you might initially think, "$700? That would buy a decent suit." But that 1880 money would be about $15,000 today. And that buying expedition was just the precursor. As commander in chief, the guy had *eighty* pairs of pants and changed several times a day. In fact, his luxurious duds spurred the nicknames "Elegant Arthur" and the "Dude President."

Arthur had always been a private man, but he was hardly a wallflower. He loved whiskey and beer, loved to party and was known to frequent nightclubs. He once told a temperance advocate who called on him at the White House, "I may be President of the United States, but my private life is nobody's damn business."

JAMES A. GARFIELD
REPUBLICAN CANDIDATE FOR PRESIDENT

CHESTER A. ARTHUR
REPUBLICAN CANDIDATE FOR VICE PRESIDENT

Candidates James Garfield and Chester A. Arthur. *Courtesy the Library of Congress.*

When he got the word in the wee hours of the morning that Garfield, who'd been shot twice the previous July, had died, he said he could only pray it was a mistake. Guests who had lingered that evening might have thought it was his regard for Garfield or the presidency. I think it was the realization that his political ride had taken a not-so-convenient turn. He had never run for office, and despite his role as part of the political machine in New York and his whiz-bang performance on the campaign trail, he was now, unexpectedly, president, imagining a not-so-distant future of hours of on-the-job-training.

Chester Arthur didn't move into the White House right away. Like President Donald Trump, he was faced with a new home that didn't meet his standards. He ordered everything removed from the residence—twenty-four wagonloads of furnishings and other items, including, it's been noted, a pair of pants that once belonged to President Lincoln. It was all carted away and sold at auction. What did Arthur do with the proceeds raised at the sacrifice of such priceless history, dating back to the time of John Adams? He hired New York artist and decorator Louis Comfort Tiffany to create more suitable digs.

Tiffany himself described some of the changes that were made:

At that time we decorated the Blue Room, the East Room, the Red Room and the Hall between the Red and East Rooms, together with the glass screen contained therein. The Blue Room, or Robin's Egg Room—as it is sometimes called—was decorated in robin's egg blue for the main color, with ornaments in a hand-pressed paper, touched out in ivory, gradually deepening as the ceiling was approached.

In the East Room, we only did the ceiling, which was done in silver, with a design in various tones of ivory.

The *Washington Evening Star* described more work undertaken by Tiffany:

They have decorated the ceiling in broad lines and masses of metal, of gold and ivory white, which, upon closer inspection, form intricate scrolls and designs, at night reflecting the rays from the three large chandeliers. There are also on the ceiling about 20 rosettes of Indian brass. The cornice and frieze are of rich designs, in golden colors, the latter being separated from the wall by a line of Indian perforated brass. The walls are of an olive golden hue, making a fine background for the paintings. The two large niches are solidly gilded, having a hammered effect, which is very much heightened by the lights and shadows caused by the leaves of the large palms which stand in majolica pots...

What will doubtless be considered the main feature of the interior improvement is the magnificent glass mosaic screen, which is expected to arrive shortly from New York. It will take the place of the present homely, ground glass partition which separates the corridor from the vestibule. It will have but two doors, the center of the screen being composed of one large panel. The center of this panel consists of a large oval, having four eagles arranged around a central smaller oval, which is a suggestion of the U.S. shield. The four rosettes, which are outside the large oval, in the corners of the panel, have the cipher U.S.A. introduced. The whole panel is filled with innumerable pieces of different hued glass and crystal.... Tiffany & Co. have never had such an opportunity of showing both sides of the glass mosaic as this will afford, and the effect produced by the lights on both sides...will doubtless be magnificent.

Arthur was known to spend lavishly and not just on furnishings, but on alcohol and food too. Our twenty-first president loved mutton chops (you are what you eat) washed down with ale. He adored macaroni pie, a casserole based on baked macaroni and cheese. Fresh fish and ice cream were some of his favorites. A typical day's fare might include coffee and a roll for breakfast; oatmeal and fish for lunch; and Rhode Island eels, salmon or oysters. Dinner might be turtle steak or roast beef with potatoes and fruit, accompanied by beer and claret— and last but not least, Nesselrode pie, a Russian dessert made with chestnuts, booze and fruit.

He had plenty of time to indulge. As president, he often arrived late to his daily duties, near 10:00 a.m. He took long lunches and lots of three-day weekends. He liked to

President Chester A. Arthur. *Courtesy the Library of Congress.*

go on fishing trips, and he loved to socialize. Arthur's wife, Ellen Lewis Herndon Arthur, died of pneumonia before her husband was elected vice president. By some accounts, Arthur fraternized frequently with a bevy of young women who were all too happy to make themselves available for his amusement. Some supporters considered this scandalous and wished the president would marry again.

There are many historians who've called him lazy, but Arthur did manage some noteworthy accomplishments as president. He signed the Pendleton Civil Service Act so government jobs would be distributed based on merit, not political connections. He vetoed the Chinese Exclusion Act, softening immigration rules. He made polygamy a federal crime and oversaw the modernization of the U.S. Navy.

It's possible that some of Arthur's laidback attitude could be attributed to illness. During his time in office, he gained nearly forty pounds, and around 1882, it was discovered he had an incurable kidney ailment, Bright's disease, whose symptoms can include pain, swelling, fatigue and hypertension. He kept the news of his condition from the public and did not seek nomination to a second term. He left the White House in March 1885, returning to New York to resume practicing law. His health continued to deteriorate. He died at home on November 18, 1886, at the

President Arthur at Yellowstone National Park. *Courtesy the Library of Congress.*

age of fifty-seven. Chester A. Arthur is gone, but the question remains: was he or wasn't he a U.S. citizen?

In 1948, a historian working on an article about the twenty-first president discovered an interesting fact: Chester A. Arthur supposedly entered Union College in 1845 at the age of sixteen, something that was impossible if he had really been born in 1830. Then there was the arrival, in 1949, of the Arthur family Bible at the New York Public Library; 1800s bibles were like early birth and death certificates, recording each family's "comings and goings." The entry for Arthur's birth indicates that he was born on October 5, 1829, which means the inscription on his tombstone is off by a year.

And here's a letter written to the Library of Congress by the president's grandson Chester A. Arthur III, back in 1961:

You may be sure that I am as interested as you are in having the Arthur papers finally come to rest in the Library of Congress. The ones that I have in my possession have travelled a good deal—over to Europe, back to Colorado, California, and now here [New York]. During his lifetime, my father would never let anyone see them—not even me. When they finally came into my possession, I was amazed that there were so few. At my father's funeral in Albany, or rather at the interment of his ashes which took place several months after his death [July 17, 1934], I enquired of all the cousins there assembled—the nieces and nephews of my grandfather, as to

The grave of President Chester A. Arthur. *Courtesy Wikimedia Commons.*

what had happened to the bulk of the papers. Charles E. McElroy, the son of Mary Arthur McElroy who was my grandfather's First Lady, tells me that the day before he died, my grandfather caused to be burned three large garbage cans, each at least four feet high, full of papers which I am sure would have thrown much light on history.

Indeed.

A MURDERER MARKS THE SPOT

*D*elia Congdon was born on Sugar Hill in the town of Wallingford, Vermont, on February 11, 1867. She was the ninth child of a ninth child, a man named James Headley Congdon II, and his wife, Artemisia Dawson. Delia's father was one of nine brothers, all of them six feet tall. When they were old enough to do the haying, neighbors would remark, smiling, that fifty-four feet of Congdons were walking out to the fields.

Through stories of her life, we know that Delia had a hearing impairment, but we don't know why. It may have been congenital, although some stories suggest it could have been caused by the scarlet fever she contracted when she was eight or nine. However she came by the deficit, with therapy being scarce in those days, she grew up with speech that was difficult to understand; eventually, she stopped talking altogether.

By the time the century turned, Delia's siblings who survived to adulthood were grown and leading independent lives, but Delia was thirty-three and had never lived alone. A 1900 census records her living on the farm with her parents. Unfortunately, just six weeks after that census was taken, Delia's father died, and her mother passed away just two years later.

With her parents gone, Delia lived for a time in town at the home of the Averys, the family of a local doctor. She attended the community's Congregational church and was active in town social life, but she missed the farm on Sugar Hill and decided she would return. She lived alone but managed not to be lonely. Her aunt and uncle had a place a short walk away, and she often went out in the afternoon, strolling to the end of her road to greet local schoolchildren who were on their way home, treating them to cookies she'd made that morning. She seemed to be living a contented life without any troubling incident, until July 24, 1908.

It was a picture-perfect Vermont day. There was a scent of clover in the air. Birds sang, and the fresh dew sparkled in the sun. Delia rose, got dressed and headed into the kitchen to begin her baking. Standing in the pantry assembling ingredients, she was clubbed in the back of the head twice with a metal rod. Her assailant ran the rod through the neck of her clothes and twisted, choking her to make sure every breath had left her body.

Late that morning, at about ten o'clock, neighbors stopping at her place noticed Delia's milk delivery still on her doorstep. They thought it peculiar and decided to enter the house to check on her. They found her lifeless body in the pantry, the floor and walls spattered with blood. She had deep gashes in her head, and it was apparent the poor woman had been sexually assaulted.

The authorities were called and began their investigation, assembling a patchwork of evidence. The first suspect held for questioning, a farmhand named Frank Rogers, turned out to be a dead end. Rogers had been working for Delia, doing some of the more physical tasks on the farm as well as some odd jobs. He was a "rough character," according to the *Burlington Free Press*, However, after an intense interview and close examination of his clothing, police decided that he could not be the culprit.

Soon they turned their attention to Elroy Kent. Kent, thirty-three years old, had recently escaped from the Vermont State Hospital for the Insane in Waterbury, Vermont. He began his criminal career at the age of seven. A habitual offender, he had been in jail or relegated to an asylum most of his life. There were those who thought his insanity claim was a sham. A deputy sheriff by the name Wilkins of Brattleboro knew Kent and had arrested him himself for several minor offenses. It was his opinion that on Kent's last lawbreaking go-round, he had faked a disorder so he could be transferred to a mental hospital, where he would have a better opportunity for escape. Be that as it may, Kent's records show no doubt whatsoever that his family suffered from a deep, shared dysfunction.

One noteworthy peculiarity of Kent's was a compulsive need to let everyone know where he'd been by carving his name or initials in things. He carved "JULY. 22. 1908" with "E. KENT" below it into the wall Buffum House, a place only three miles from Sugar Hill. On the twenty-third, the night authorities believe he spent at Delia's farm, he carved "E.K." on the wall inside the barn.

Wallingford, Vermont, early 1900s. *Courtesy the University of Vermont.*

Sugar Hill, in East Wallingford, Vermont. *Courtesy Thea Lewis.*

These carvings were just one of the clues police had regarding his likelihood as Delia's assailant. As was later revealed in the July 23 *Wallingford Times,* authorities also knew that a stranger fitting Kent's description had stopped at the home of her neighbors, the Spragues, asking for a job. While talking to the Spragues, he noticed Delia working in her yard and asked the boys who she was; then he far overshot the bounds of polite conversation by telling them the kinds of things he'd like to do with her if he could get her alone. Her protective neighbors set him straight, letting him know that they would "shoot full of holes" anyone who touched her.

Once they figured out it was Kent they were looking for, the town and the state as a whole began one of the biggest manhunts Vermont had ever seen. Every available officer in Rutland County and as many armed farmers as could be assembled scoured the woods looking for the escapee. Bloodhounds from the kennels of a breeder named Manning Cleveland of Poughkeepsie, New York, were brought to join in the search.

A flurry of Elwood Kent sightings began. With the hysteria surrounding the murder and the circumstances of the criminal's escape, they were numerous and didn't always make sense. It was reported that Mrs. L.H. Pratt was chased by a strange man, presumed to be Kent, while driving home on the morning of July 28. That same day, two boys reported seeing someone they also thought could be Kent, naked and sitting under a tree munching on green apples.

There were so many Elroy Kent sightings that the *Burlington Free Press* editors instructed their reporters to keep a close watch. On August 7, 1908, the paper ran a slew of humorous Elroy Kent "sightings" creating tongue-in-cheek special reports of their own. A partial list finds the perp seen swimming fast in Lake Memphremagog, up in Newport—so fast that the initials "E.K." were created in his wake. Then he was seen drinking from Highgate Springs and, after that, waving from Rock Dunder in the middle of Lake Champlain. Particularly amusing is the one where he has a get-rich-quick scheme and is seen with a shovel mining for copper in Bolton. Also strikingly vivid is a sighting that has him shrieking at the announcement by a band at Battery Park that its next number would be the "Merry Widow Waltz." My favorite fictitious Elroy Kent sighting, though, is the one here:

WINOOSKI IS INNOCENT
(Special)
Winooski, August 7th—To the lasting credit of this bustling town, Elroy Kent is not, and never has been here.

In the village of East Wallingford. *Courtesy Thea Lewis.*

The search went on. At one point, bloodhounds picked up a scent that led to the home of Mrs. Rollin Flanders. The place was searched, but there was no trace of "E.K." on the premises. Several other houses were searched, too, based on the nose work of Mr. Cleveland's bloodhounds, but eventually the trail went cold. A fifty-dollar reward was offered for information on Kent's whereabouts. That same week, nervous trustees at Waterbury mental hospital began making plans to reconstruct the facility to make escape more difficult for wards of the state.

In August, there was a glimmer of hope and more rumored sightings. Workmen saw a man believed to be Kent hiding out in the woods in Dorset, but when they tried to apprehend him, he fled. It was thought that Kent had enjoyed dinner in Mount Tabor with a man named Martin Sargent, who was unaware of the manhunt, and also that a man with blood-spattered clothes had been spotted in Pittsford, Vermont. Both stories proved to be false.

Then, on October 21, in Pittsfield, Massachusetts, police handled a report of a stolen bicycle. The thief, who called himself William Allen, had attempted to resell the bike for two dollars and was caught and questioned. He named a string of places he'd recently been employed: Schenectady, New York, as well as Springfield, Holyoke and Greenfield, Massachusetts. Too many things about his story didn't match up. The police called the Waterbury asylum and spoke with Dr. D.D. Grout. They provided a description the man, causing Dr. Grout to believe he wasn't William Allen at all but rather the infamous Elroy Kent. A contingent from Vermont that included States Attorney R.A. Lawrence of Rutland traveled to Pittsfield to make a positive ID, and E.K. found himself headed back to the Green Mountain State, to be detained in the house of correction in Rutland, where he would await his trial for the murder of Delia Congdon.

On November 18, Kent was transferred back to the hospital in Waterbury so that doctors could make an assessment of his mental state. It was judged he was fit to stand trial. In March 1909, Kent was finally scheduled to go before the court, although it took a while to select a jury. Twenty-eight men were rejected during voir dire, or preliminary examination, because there had been so much talk and so many opinions expressed publicly about the murder and the defendant.

The first court date was April 1, and Elroy Kent had entered a plea of "not guilty." The state brought its first witnesses. When it called the Sprague family to testify, there was plenty to say. There was the boys' conversation with Kent; the body-sized depression discovered in the hay in Delia's barn, indicating someone had bedded down there; and a strange pouch of tobacco that turned up in the stall. Mrs. Sprague testified that the drawers in the Congdon home had been ransacked. Then there was the other evidence in the barn, "E.K." initials carved in the wall and fresh wood shavings on the dirt floor. Kent listened quietly to the testimony. It was noted that he looked very different from before he went to Waterbury. He had gained a noticeable amount of weight and shaved his mustache, making him look younger. He spent most of the trial with his eyes half closed. It was thought that he might fall asleep at any moment.

Upon questioning, he admitted to carving his initials in various locations around the state but denied ever being on Sugar Hill. After a long period of testimony, Dr. Grout of the mental facility, where Kent had been housed, testified for the defense and swore the opinion that Kent was a moral imbecile.

Judge E.L. Watermen felt the need to exclude women from the courtroom during the next phase of testimony and evidence exhibited by Dr. B.H. Stone of the State Laboratory of Hygiene. Stone showed those who were inside the courtroom Delia's bloodstained dress and described the state in which she was found. Then Deputy Sheriff Allen Leonard and Herbert Savery, who was there to corroborate his testimony, told those assembled that Kent had confessed to the murder shortly after being brought back from Pittsfield and wasn't shy about telling Leonard what he had done to Delia, admitting he ended up killing her because she made a noise and he was afraid of being discovered. The prosecution appeared to more than make its case. There was motive, opportunity and even a confession. They had the bloody clothing and the laboratory results. In closing arguments, the prosecutor's words rang out in the courtroom: "First she was fighting for her honor, then she was fighting for her life, and anyone who murders in the act of rape deserves to hang."

When the trial concluded on Wednesday, April 9, 1909, the jury issued a guilty verdict—assault and first-degree murder. Kent's punishment would be death by hanging. The *Wallingford Times* reported that "after the verdict, Kent was led back to his cell by sheriff Leonard of Wallingford. Kent asked for a cigar, lit it and said, 'Well...let them hang me. I don't care.'"

"I guess you'll holler when they get the rope around your neck," Leonard replied.

"No, I won't," said Kent. "I'll take my medicine."

There was still one move to be played. Kent's lawyer, Ernest O'Brien, petitioned the state Supreme Court for a new trial, based on what the defense considered a discrepancy between the carvings that were found and a signature by the defendant made in pencil. The Supreme Court examined the findings in question and ruled them admissible, pointing to the continuity of Kent's use of periods after the month and day numbers present in his writings and carvings. There was no error in the previous court proceedings, it said. The verdict would stand.

Elroy Kent was transferred to the state penitentiary in Windsor. In 1910, efforts were made to commute his sentence from "death" to "life in prison," but the move failed in the legislature and got no help from Governor John A. Mead. An execution was set for January 5, 1912. Despite the brutality of the crime, there were plenty of Vermonters dead set against the idea. Vermont has never been too keen on capital punishment. The last time a prisoner was executed in the state was 1954, and the legislature moved to abolish capital punishment in 1972.

At 1:18 p.m. on Friday, January 5, 1912, the stage was set for Kent to meet his maker. He stood with the gallows rope around his neck and his feet planted firmly on the trapdoor below. His execution would mark the first time the Vermont Department of Corrections would activate its new electrical trapdoor system, a panel with six buttons, so six individuals could apply the fickle finger of fate and have the peace of mind of never knowing whether they were responsible for initiating the sequence.

As the buttons were pressed, the trapdoor opened and Kent's body dropped. Then the unthinkable happened. The rope broke, and Kent's body fell to the floor below. Nobody checked to see that Kent was dead. Instead, they tied the rope over the gallows and allowed him to hang for an additional half hour, just to make sure. At 1:45 p.m., a doctor examined him and discovered that he had been killed in the initial fall when the rope broke.

Newspapers had been barred from the execution because of a similar incident in 1905, when Mary Rogers, a murderer from Montpelier, died in the same manner. One theory, in a case of true "gallows humor" after the Kent debacle, was that they were using the same rope.

I think that if it weren't for bad luck, the Kent family would have had no luck at all. Just four months after Elroy Kent was convicted of murder, the decomposed body of his sixty-year-old father, George A. Kent, who had been missing since the middle of summer, was found by two young boys near his farm in Townshend. Reports said his decomposed body, found in a ravine, had been gnawed on by animals. The death was ruled suspicious. Authorities questioned his son Fred, who had, like his brother Elroy, been in and out of the hospital in Waterbury. At the time of their inquiry, Fred was a "guest" of the town Newfane, Vermont, jailed on a burglary charge. He was indicted by a grand jury, found to be insane and sent back to Waterbury. A December 13, 1911 story in the *Burlington Free Press* revealed that Fred Kent, who worked in the hospital boiler room, had escaped the facility at seven o'clock in the morning, only to return at nine o'clock that night. The article noted that Fred was "considered not violent" but also mentioned that "during a period of a previous escape from the hospital, he is thought to have killed his father."

He claimed to have hidden in the coal shed during his fourteen-hour absence. I wonder what he was really up to?

GREEDY JOHN HUBBARD

I love ghost stories and urban legends, and one of Vermont's most famous is the tale of Black Agnes. Agnes isn't really black— and, technically, isn't a woman. It's a cemetery monument that carries a curse that some say could cost you your life.

On January 29, 1890, word traveled to Vermont that Fanny Hubbard Kellogg had passed away in New York City. She and her husband, Martin, who had predeceased her by just a few months, were childless and had decided to leave their entire estate, more than $300,000, to the City of Montpelier. The will directed that $55,000 should be used to benefit the cemetery, and the rest would go to the creation of a public library in their name.

Fanny's nephew, John Hubbard, got his nose all out of joint over this state of affairs. He had been convinced that he would inherit at least part of the estate. He was a bachelor, with no savings, and was still living with his parents. He challenged the will with the assistance of Fanny's only other living relatives, his own blind father and a doddering uncle, who had been signatories.

When the will entered probate, the two older men seemed confused—it was a *will* they had signed? Imagine that. They claimed that they hadn't realized the document's intent. The judge bought their story and ruled the paper invalid.

Montpelier officials were hopping mad. They filed a suit in the Vermont Supreme Court to try to force Hubbard to give them their money. Four years after Fanny died, not long before the court was expected to hand down a ruling, it was still anybody's guess who would win. That's when the town decided to compromise with Hubbard. He'd get to keep the bulk of the money but had to promise to pay for the library, which was expected to cost in the neighborhood of $30,000.

He agreed, but the verbal tussling wasn't over. When the city hired Amos P. Cutting of Worcester, Massachusetts, to design the building, and his plans revealed it would be called the Kellogg-Hubbard Library, people were beside themselves that shady John Hubbard could cause so much grief, shortchange the town and still manage to get his name over the door.

Hubbard may have gotten away with the money, and the honor, but he didn't get to enjoy it long. He contracted liver cancer, a turn some people considered payback. To further bolster that opinion, on the morning he died a memorable summer storm roared through the county, as though God himself was venting his wrath on John Hubbard.

John W. Burgess, a professor at Columbia University who spent summers in Montpelier, had been a good friend to Martin Kellogg, as well as someone who'd been infuriated by the way Kellogg's nephew had manipulated the inheritance to his favor. He wrote of Hubbard's end:

> *At midnight the hurricane burst upon us; great trees swayed and houses trembled; torrential rain fell; the lightning was so incessant that it seemed no longer night but brilliant day; and the incessant roar of thunder was like the discharge of a thousand cannons. At daybreak it ceased.... Word ran through the town that, in the midst of the tor-nado, the spirit of Hubbard had departed.*

Hubbard died on July 17, 1899, at the age of fifty-two and was interred at Green Mount Cemetery. His trustees had been instructed to erect a monument over his final resting place in the family plot, telling them they could spend an amount not less than $5,000 but not more than $10,000. The resultant memorial, designed by sculptor Karl Bitter, is one of Vermont's most striking and infamous. The mournful, life-sized figure draped in a shroud is meant to be the figure of Thanatos, a character from Greek mythology, who is death personified. Legend says that "Black Agnes" has tempted many a visitor to sit on its lap. You might want to resist the urge. If you don't, you could end up dead.

Green Mount Cemetery, established in 1834, is filled with wondrous and compelling monuments, among them the carved image of Margaret Pitkin,

The Kellogg-Hubbard Library. *Courtesy Wikimedia Commons.*

Black Agnes. *Courtesy Chad Abramovich.*

known as "Little Margaret"; loyal "Ned the Dog"; and William Stowell's "Hand Carved Stairs." None of them offers the paranormal punch of Black Agnes, who also goes by the nickname "Black Aggie."

There's a decades-old story of three teenagers who sat on Black Agnes during a full moon, trying to show one another how brave they were. When nothing happened, they laughed about it on the way home, sure that they'd put one over on old Aggie. One week later, one boy fell and shattered his leg. Another died in a tragic car crash. The third drowned.

You may be surprised to learn that Vermont isn't the only state with a "Black Agnes." There are similar statues in Washington, D.C.; Chicago; Maryland; and West Virginia. They're all thought to bring bad luck.

In Pikesville, Maryland's Druid Ridge Cemetery, the Black Agnes at the grave of General Felix Agnus, who died on Halloween, is supposedly haunted by the spirit of a mistreated wife who lay beneath the statue's feet. The statue's eyes are said to glow red at midnight. People say that if you're pregnant and sit in the lap of the Agnes in Washington, D.C., you'll miscarry. Some say the statue will come to life and crush you in its stony embrace. And just like Beetlejuice, Black Aggie comes with a warning about saying her name three times—so don't, especially not while looking in the mirror. Legend says that if you do, a dark angel will pull your soul straight to hell.

APPARENTLY YOU AIN'T PARENTS

*M*other's Day was created in 1908 by a woman named Anna Jarvis, who worshiped her own mother, Ann, for many reasons. She was especially proud of her mother's tender care of the troops during the Civil War and for the fact that she sweetly sought to foster peace between mothers of Union and Confederate soldiers by creating something called "Mother's Friendship Day."

By the time Mother's Day became an official holiday in 1914, Ann Jarvis had begun to regret her efforts to designate a special day for moms because of how steeped in commercialism the observance quickly became. However you feel about celebrating the holiday, you can probably agree that mothering isn't easy, and most moms deserve some recognition. Still, there are some who make Joan Crawford in *Mommie Dearest* look like Mother of the Year. The same can be said for dads. Most are great and rightly get credit for teaching kids how to catch a ball, how to survive their dad's goofy jokes and how to know when to stop kicking the car seat in front of them. (If I have to stop this car...!) But there are also guys who should probably remain childless. Some of them make sure of it. Here are some Vermonters never destined to be named "Parent of the Year."

HANNAH PARKER

On June 14, 1846, in Coventry, Vermont, a town best known for a weekend-long festival hosted by the rock band Phish back in the summer of 2004, Hannah Parker murdered her small son.

Now, nineteenth-century rural life in the Northeast Kingdom—or NEK, as it's sometimes called—could be harsh, especially for a woman. Winters are long and cold. There were endless, backbreaking chores, plus expectations and social conventions we can only imagine. But what kind of stresses, strains and demands would cause a woman to take her toddler out walking in the middle of June, bind his leg to his neck with one of her garters and throw him into the region's Black River?

As the tale goes, Hannah, who also went by the name "Stickney," had been married once or twice. It was questioned at the time of the trial whether she knew who her child's father was. One thing was sure: she had no partner at the time of the murder and no means of support.

Burlington's Home for Friendless Women, a place designed to assist women who were pregnant and unmarried or deserted by their husbands and families, wasn't established until 1890. Back in those days, there were no social programs to speak of. Stories of the incident indicate that Hannah saw the child as an anchor, preventing her from finding a place to stay or future employment. The court believed that these factors "overcame the maternal instinct," making her think that murdering her son was her only option. She was arrested and jailed, tried and then, though the narrative doesn't offer up any details, tried again. Eventually, she was found guilty, but the court reversed the ruling. In all, she spent about eight years in jail. When she was released, it was noted that her punishment was sufficient, as she had committed the crime "in great weakness of mind and extreme desperation of circumstances."

EMELINE MEAKER

Alice Meaker and Elmer Meaker were from Charlotte, Vermont. In 1873, their father died, and six years later, their poor, struggling mother sent them to live in an overcrowded poor farm. Soon afterward, their mother ended up married again, to a man with the surname Germaine. She moved to South Burlington with him, leaving the children wards of the state.

The overseer managed to place Elmer in a home with the Sisters of Mercy in Burlington. Alice, then thirteen, went to live with Horace Meaker, the children's much older half-brother, and his wife, Emeline, who made their home in Duxbury, Vermont.

Horace and Emeline were in their mid-forties and both quite deaf. Struggling farmers, they had raised two children of their own: Louis Almon Meaker, nineteen, and Nellie, eighteen, a schoolteacher who was no longer living at home. The state paid the couple $400 for Alice's support, but Emeline was not happy with the arrangement and made sure Alice knew it. She called her "little bitch" and "that thing," constantly berated the slight, timid child and made her do work that would have exhausted a farmhand. She liked to teach Alice lessons through the use of physical punishment, but after a while, she stopped requiring a reason and just hit the girl whenever she felt like it.

In the spring of 1880, the Meakers moved to a house closer to the Waterbury/Duxbury line. Alice moved, too, and her abuse at the hands of Emeline became even worse than before. She was scolded and beaten on a regular basis. Emeline would beat her horribly with a broom, a stick or whatever else was at hand. Emeline was quite literally deaf to the little girl's screams, as she had a severe hearing impairment.

Neighbors said that the child's cries could be heard from half a mile away, but while many in the small community of Duxbury were aware of the abuse, no one bothered to do anything about it. Some said that even though they hated the way the little girl was treated, they thought coming to her defense might only make things worse.

On April 21, 1880, Emeline decided to bring the situation to a close. She waited until her husband fell asleep and then convinced her son, Louis, nineteen years old, to help her carry out her plan. She told him to hire a team of horses, and he did. The two went to the room where Alice slept, threw a bag over her head and carried her struggling and screaming little body out of the house. At about 10:00 p.m., Louis drove his mother and Alice toward town. Just outside the village, he took a bottle of sweetened water mixed with the poison strychnine his mother had told him to buy at a druggist in Waterbury and poured it into a mug with some water from a spring from the side of the road. They fed the water to Alice and drove toward Stowe, waiting for the chemical to take effect.

The hour-long drive was agonizing, with the girl crying out for her mother. They had to stop the horses under a covered bridge and cover her mouth to muffle her screams. She flailed so violently in her agony that Louis, having

Stereograph view, Duxbury, Vermont, 1875. *Courtesy Library of Congress.*

to recall it, later said, "I shall be glad when I am dead." When the girl finally stopped writhing and spasming, they hid her lifeless body in the swamp.

The following day, a Sunday, neighbors could not help but notice that Alice was not at home. Their questions regarding her whereabouts went unanswered, and their suspicions caused them to alert Sheriff Atherton of Waterbury. On Monday, as he began to interview the family, a nervous Louis broke his silence first, laying the blame for the girl's death completely on his mother. He agreed to take the sheriff to where the body was hidden. Once they had retrieved it, he tried to put it under the wagon seat, but it was stiff and didn't fit. They had to make the trip back to town with the dead girl between them, with Louis holding her head upright, her long auburn hair falling over his shoulder.

But the very next day, Louis retracted his confession, saying that he alone was at fault and that his mother had nothing to do with Alice's murder. It was thought at the time that the boy recanted due to fear of his mother's wrath. Whatever his reasons, he stuck with this new version of the tale, preventing the state from using his original confession as evidence. In the end, he and his mother were both indicted.

Once imprisoned, Emeline savagely attacked a sheriff and tried to set fire to the jail. It was believed she hoped to be found insane so she could evade her punishment. Louis Meaker was sentenced to death by hanging, but the sentence was commuted and changed to a life term. He died in the State Prison in Windsor on December 5, 1893, of tuberculosis at the age of thirty-two.

As for Emeline, she did hang on March 30, 1883, the very first woman in Vermont to do so. Her last meal was two hardboiled eggs, two slices of toast, a potato, a doughnut and a cup of coffee. To prepare for the execution, Emeline parted her hair in the middle and drew it over her temples in a style that was different from the style spectators were accustomed to. When someone said she looked no older than sixteen, she laughed and agreed she did look pretty good.

Escorted to the gallows and seeing the chair on the scaffold, she walked purposefully toward it, showing no emotion. She looked a bit pale and resigned, but that was all. People couldn't believe how she was holding up. In fact, hers was called one of the most remarkable executions of modern times. The *Burlington Free Press* noted that "such wonderful nerve and composure on the scaffold is seldom seen."

The chaplain kneeled to offer her a prayer, but the sheriff, because of her deafness, didn't read her warrant of execution. Instead he handed her a slip of paper. It read, "Emeline L. Meaker....Have you anything to say why the sentence of the law should not now be executed upon you? There is now an opportunity." Her answer, "May God forgive you all for hanging me, an innocent woman." She raised her captured hands and pointed toward the deputy. "I am as innocent as that man standing there."

Vermont State Prison, Windsor, Vermont. *Courtesy the University of Vermont.*

They secured her ankles, and she momentarily cried out, "Oh, Christ… Oh, Christ." Then her face was covered. It was over almost before anyone knew what had happened, at 1:36 p.m.

EUGENE CLIFFORD

Fathers are not above infanticide. In the early 1840s, a man named Eugene Clifford, a deserter from the British army, ended up in Franklin County, Vermont, in the town of Fairfield.

The town had a hard time warming up to the guy. He had proven himself disloyal, and they found him a bit of a blowhard. Still, something about him managed to catch the eye of a local widow. She was an Irishwoman named Elizabeth Gilmore, who was financially well off, with her own home and a fifty-acre farm. Somehow, Clifford enticed her into marriage. It was not a happy union for Clifford, who felt constrained by the bonds of matrimony. They had a child, a daughter, which made him even more glum. The couple argued about many things, but mostly about his wandering eye. Clifford had zeroed in on a particular woman, one who, like Elizabeth, also had a fair amount of money and land. A bit younger, she lived on the other side of the lake. On a crisp, cloudless Sunday, October 16, 1842, Clifford came in from his chores and surprised Elizabeth by telling her that he intended to take the family on a boat ride.

Because the air was cool, Elizabeth went to get a scarf for the baby and one for herself—her prized paisley shawl, which had been a gift from her family in Ireland. She bundled herself and the baby into the boat, ready to face the October winds, and Eugene paddled away from the shore. Several people from the town saw them leave and waved happy goodbyes to the handsome family. But several hours later, the boat drifted in, with a scraggly, water-soaked Eugene inside. He was in a terrible state, moaning and crying bitterly.

When neighbors calmed him enough to make out his words, he told them that once he'd gotten his little family to the middle of the lake, a strong wind started up, rocking the boat. He said Elizabeth moved to wrap the shawl tighter around the baby, and the boat tipped, throwing the two into the cold water. He searched and searched, he said. He was afraid they must have drowned.

Fairfield Pond. *Courtesy of the Town of Fairfield, Vermont.*

Example of an 1800s paisley shawl. *Courtesy the Philadelphia Museum of Art.*

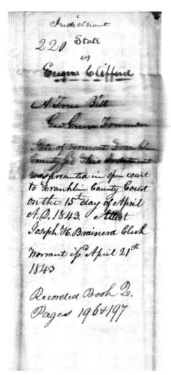

Eugene Clifford indictment.
Courtesy the Burlington Free Press.

There were still a few hours of daylight left. Neighbor notified neighbor, until nearly the whole town was searching for Eugene Clifford's family. The next day, they searched again and were saddened by the end result. Elizabeth and her child were found not far from the lakeshore, several feet apart. Both were dead.

During the course of planning the double funeral, questions began to mount about the sincerity of Eugene's grief. A gentleman who had been drinking fireside at a local inn recalled a conversation in which Clifford had drunkenly (and jokingly, the fellow thought at the time) mentioned his wife's wealth and wondered, if she should die, whether he would inherit free and clear and therefore be set for life.

Then there was the mystery of the prized shawl. Women who knew Elizabeth knew she would have had it with her that day. But it wasn't with her body when she was found. When one neighbor innocently asked where Eugene thought it might be, he snapped at her, "How the Devil should I know?"

Mrs. Abigail Marvin was the closest friend Elizabeth had. She could not shake the idea that something was very wrong with Clifford's story. One night, she had a dream. In it, she traveled the lake and then crossed through fields and woods and meadows until she got to a place with a hollow tree, not far from Fairfield Pond. In the tree was a flat rock, and under the rock was the prized shawl. Mrs. Marvin woke up frantic and told her husband that they had to find this place. He assured her that it was only a dream, the result of grief and an overactive imagination.

Abigail was positive that the dream was a message. She found a neighbor, Orsamus Bailey, who agreed to go searching with her. They followed the path the dream indicated and indeed found the shawl. They brought the evidence back to town. Clifford was locked up, tried and convicted of double homicide. To this day, Fairfield Pond is known as Dream Lake.

MILDRED BREWSTER GOT A GUN

*L*ove triangles are rarely satisfying—believe me, I speak from experience. Relationships are tricky enough when it's one-on-one. Add a third person to the equation and things get really nutty. That's what happened in Montpelier back in 1897, when a young, already discontented woman named Mildred Brewster set her sights on a stonecutter named Jack Wheeler.

Mildred Brewster, born Lena Merilla Brewster on June 5, 1876, grew up in rural Huntington, Vermont, the youngest child of Wesley Brewster and his wife, Emma. Brewster was a farmer, successful and well-to-do. When his wife passed away, leaving him with the care of Mildred and the farm, he did the best he could to satisfy the child's needs, but she had a restless, inconsistent temperament. He couldn't make her happy in Huntington, so he agreed to let her go to live in Burlington, a place that had more to offer in the way of diversions and opportunities for a productive life.

Mildred attended Burlington High School, but it seemed that didn't suit her either. She didn't graduate. Instead, she found work as a waitress at a local restaurant. After a while, she grew dissatisfied with Burlington too. She ended up back in Huntington, where it was suggested she teach school. She accepted the position, but her impatient temperament won out and she didn't last long in the position. After life in the city, a small town like Huntington was not where she wanted to be.

At twenty, with dwindling prospects, she decided to relocate to Vermont's capital. Montpelier was a beautiful, bustling city, close enough to home and her father, who hoped to keep an eye on her. It was as good place as any to make a fresh start.

She found a room that suited her, boarding at the home of Mr. and Mrs. John F. Goodenough, and got a job at a local tailor shop, Ledden and Campbell. Her life and place in society in the capital city appeared to be proceeding normally. A *Burlington Free Press* roundup of Montpelier social happenings printed on October 31, 1896, noted, "Miss Mildred Brewster goes to-day to Burlington for a few days visit with friends."

An outsider might think that her life was chugging along, but for Mildred, a piece of the puzzle was missing: she had no suitors. To say that she was fixated on this would have put it mildly.

When she met Jack Wheeler, who rented a room in the same boardinghouse, she was smitten. Twenty-two years old with a body forged by cutting stone, he was a catch by anyone's standards. But Jack wasn't interested in Mildred, at least not, as some would say, in that way. He had set his sights on another, younger girl, Anna Wheeler. Anna was a seventeen-year-old East Montpelier girl. Although she had the same surname, the two were not related. Jack left the boardinghouse, moving in with family. Mildred, once encouraged by his brief show of affection, did everything she could to keep his attention.

Montpelier, early 1900s. *Courtesy the University of Vermont.*

For a few weeks leading up to the end of May and Decoration Day, observers noticed that Mildred had not been herself. She had lost her job at the tailor shop, and on top of having her advances ignored by Jack, that failure was more than she could bear. It was expected that she would go back to her family home in Huntington in just a few days' time. Then she learned that Jack had arranged to take Anna to the upcoming Decoration Day celebration in nearby Barre on May 30. Mildred had hoped that he would be inviting her, and upon hearing this, she grew even more agitated.

On the Friday evening before the holiday, she'd been heard making what people assumed were idle threats, saying that she would get even with Jack for toying with her affections. She even hung around the Armory, where he was engaged in rifle practice, waiting for him to come out. People wondered, in retrospect, if she'd been planning to take out her frustrations by shooting him then and there.

On the morning of May 30, there was a light drizzle falling over Montpelier. Mildred put on her black dress and raincoat and set out to do some target shooting with her .32-caliber Ives and Johnson revolver. There's speculation over whether she meant to settle the situation once and for all or simply intended to scare young Anna and then turn the gun on herself, but either way, she ended up walking up College Street toward Main to the home of her rival. The two women spent nearly an hour in heated conversation. Mildred said that she had a claim to Jack. Anna insisted that was not the case. At about 8:00 a.m., they were seen walking together back down College Street toward Jack's house on Sibley Avenue. Jack's brother spotted the two women and called to him. Jack ran to the door, realizing that this could only mean trouble. As he stood watching from the front of the house, the two women left College Street, turning into a field, where they were hidden from his view. Once they were in the ravine, Mildred pulled out her revolver, shot Anna and then herself.

Jack and his brother ran to the ravine. A professor, D.S. Blanpied, had seen the two women walking. Hearing the shots, he assumed the situation was dire. He called the police, who responded, surveyed the scene and took statements from the many witnesses. Mildred had shot the girl behind her right ear and then shot herself *through* the right ear. Their heads lay only about a foot apart. Both women were unconscious. Brain matter and blood oozed from Anna's head onto the dirt below. The bodies were removed to nearby Heaton Hospital, where Anna was pronounced dead at 1:30 p.m.

Mildred was in rough shape, clinging to life. She regained consciousness and at least once cried out, "Oh, why didn't I die?" It was reported that hospital attendants were growing tired of constantly being pulled away from their duties to answer telephone calls about her condition. Mildred lingered on the brink of death for weeks, with a bullet still in her head. Finally, she began to rebound, but her recovery was long. She might feel better in the morning after a long night's rest, but by the end of the day, she would be in excruciating pain. Doctors failed to remove the bullet until January of the next year. Mildred suffered permanent disfigurement to the right side of her face.

Her father and her brother, Carlos, had arrived from Huntington as soon as they heard the news. Wesley Brewster was determined that his daughter wouldn't die on the gallows. He began making calls, looking for the best attorney money could buy. He retained Frank Plumley, a lawyer from Washington County who was a graduate of Norwich University and who would go on to become a member of the U.S. House of Representatives. Plumley was highly intelligent, well respected by the courts and a brilliant orator. It didn't long for him to discover that Mildred's family tree revealed more than its fair share of relatives with mental illnesses and deaths by suicide.

Her friends and coworkers were willing to testify that she had long been emotionally unstable. Also, there was the idea that Mildred Brewster was "afflicted with the insanity of a seduced woman." She had been trifled with by Jack Wheeler. Plumley would use this information as he pieced together his defense: innocent by reason of insanity. It would be a landmark case.

The story captured the headlines. The coverage was some of the most extensive seen locally. Advertising posters were published reminding people to keep up to date with news of this scandalous trial about a triangulated relationship gone terribly wrong. People didn't need much reminding. The testimony was chock full of sensational tidbits, capturing the interest of readers far and wide. *The Day*, a paper in New London, Connecticut, ran the headline, "SOCIETY GIRL TRIED FOR MURDER."

Mildred's poor father was questioned regarding the mental illness on his dead wife's side of the family. His departed spouse, Emma Brewster, was the daughter of Arnold Sherman, a Washington County farmer who was believed to be "deranged." In just one incident of peculiar behavior, he bought a farm for $6,000, only to sell it a few days later for $2,500. He died at age sixty-six, a suicide. Mildred's mother, a "sensitive" woman and easily disturbed, was dealt an irreparable blow when one of her small children was accidentally scalded to death. Afterward, her behavior grew increasingly strange, particularly while she was carrying Mildred. She was

Washington County
Courthouse. *Courtesy
Wikimedia Commons.*

despondent and threatened to kill herself. Brewster told the court that she
had to be watched closely by family and friends, and anything in the house
she might use to try to poison herself was hidden in the barn. Once Mildred
was born, Emma paid almost no attention to her, and right up to her death
from congestive heart failure at the age of forty-seven, she never treated
the girl the way she did their other children. It was noted that Mildred's
maternal aunt, Molly Farr, had also been ruled insane and relegated to the
state asylum.

Mildred's father went on to describe his daughter's childhood, filled
with "fits" and fainting spells that would leave her weak and sleepy. At
some point, she was the victim of an emotional shock that rendered her
mute for a long period afterward. By the time she was fifteen, she was
threatening suicide and had to be watched carefully. Mr. Brewster told
of his visits with his daughter during her incarceration at the hospital in
Waterbury and how she begged him to bring morphine when he came so
she could take her own life.

There was testimony from Dr. F.W. Page, superintendent of the state hospital in Waterbury. He'd had many conversations with Mildred during which she insisted, morosely, that she did not intend to kill Anna Wheeler. She only meant to harm herself. She confided a sexual relationship with Jack Wheeler, something Jack initially denied, even going so far as to get the owners of the boardinghouse to vouch for him. They made statements saying that Mildred had been obsessed with the man but that he had not shown any interest in her. Later, Jack admitted that they did have sexual relations. Letters the two had written each other while he was out of town were provided as evidence.

Jack tried to make it seem like Mildred had other sexual partners. She denied this, insisting that there had only been Jack. She said she had loved him then and still, even though he wasn't worthy of it. As it turned out, Mildred probably was, or led to believe she was, secretly engaged to Jack Wheeler. When it finally came out that she had been pregnant and had aborted her baby at her lover's request, public opinion began to turn. The court heard how, in hospital interviews, she'd been asked if Jack Wheeler knew she intended to take her own life. She said yes, that had threatened to do so several times. It seems he either didn't take her threats seriously or just didn't care. He'd misused her and then became engaged to Anna behind her back. It was easy to see how a woman could lose her mind.

Mildred, when she appeared in court, sat in a wheelchair, looking dazed and sad. The right side of her face was mutilated. She cried during witnesses' testimony. Often, the courtroom was filled with sobbing women who were sympathetic to her predicament.

In the end, the jury of twelve, all male, also sided with the defendant. On May 5, 1898, Mildred was acquitted and sent back to the Asylum for the Insane in Waterbury. It was written that Mildred didn't seem to feel one way or another about the verdict. In fact, when she left court with the sheriff, she walked slowly past the crowds of curious people lining the street to catch a glimpse, acting like she didn't even see them.

She stayed at the hospital for over a decade, even though she was deemed sane enough to be released in 1905. Unfortunately, her father had passed away, and there was nowhere for her to go. She paid for her room and board at the hospital by doing work in the sewing room. She was no trouble, but authorities feared that the longer she spent in confinement, the less "resourceful" she would be on the outside. She did allow herself to be released in 1908, into the custody of a childhood friend, Mrs. William Ross, but she soon began exhibiting "troubling behavior" and was returned. It was another eight years before she was released again, this time into the custody of a nurse who had befriended her during her incarceration.

For some time, Mildred had been the subject of a disagreement between a Dr. W.D. Berry of Burlington, who had spent five years observing her, and Dr. D.D. Grout, the new supervisor of the state asylum. Berry believed that the woman was sane and didn't pose any danger to society. Grout, with another member of the hospital staff weighing in, said that her low

Mildred Brewster. *Courtesy the* Burlington Free Press.

intelligence and temperament might cause her to go off the deep end and commit "some untoward act."

When a home was offered in Bellingham, Washington, a safe distance from Vermont, with a nurse she had met while at the hospital, Mildred was released and traveled there with Washington County sheriff Frank Tracy. In all, she had spent nearly twenty years in the state hospital. She never married and lived in the Washington State area until she died at on April 27, 1942, at the age of sixty-five.

THE WITCH OF WALL STREET

I consider myself to be pretty frugal. Gifts to family and friends for birthdays or other occasions are not accompanied by a store-bought card, and I've been known to make my own curly bows out of wrapping paper. Most of my clothes are thrift shop finds, and I can't resist rehabbing items I find free by the side of the road. I'm sure there are times my husband enters our garage and thinks he's walked into an episode of the TV show *Hoarders*.

But there are times when I draw the line. I like a nice meal out every so often, I won't buy used underwear and—to paraphrase the character Monica from *Friends* in a scene where she introduces herself to her newborn nephew—"I will always have wine."

There's a difference between scrimping a bit and being obsessive where saving is concerned. In the case of Hetty Green of Bellows Falls, Vermont, also known as the "Witch of Wall Street," that difference made her the richest woman in America.

Henrietta Howland Robinson was born on November 21, 1834, in New Bedford, Massachusetts. Her father and grandfather, Edward Mott Robinson and Gideon Howland, were whaling merchants. At the time, whale oil was a necessary fuel, used for lighting lamps and making candles and soap. The family, who were of the Quaker faith, were wealthy but typically taciturn New Englanders.

Hetty, firstborn and female, was unlucky in winning her family's attention. When she was only two, her brother, Isaac, was born but lived only a few weeks. In her grief, Hetty's mother was incapable of handling the toddler, so her father, never keen on having a girl in the first place, packed her off to live with an unmarried aunt. Hetty was a bright, pretty child with angelic blue eyes and fair skin who was often given nickels for her good behavior. She was both privileged and neglected at the same time.

Her family may not have recognized her full worth until it coincided with their appreciation for the value of a dollar. They were pleased when Hetty, at just eight years of age, marched downtown to the local bank and opened her own savings account. The story was repeated among family and friends, and Hetty's stature in their eyes grew.

Used to having her own way at home, she often found conforming to the world outside the family difficult. At ten, she was enrolled in school in Sandwich, Massachusetts, and quickly discovered that the food she was expected to eat was not to her liking. She turned up her nose at the first meal she was offered. On her next visit to the dining room, she was shocked to find her previously unfinished plate, which she again refused. The third meal was served, and it looked hauntingly familiar. Rather than reject the plate a third time, she ate it. Decades later, she said it was the best thing that could have happened to her. It probably helped prepare her for the frugal meals she made much later, on a hotplate in the boardinghouse rooms she rented. (As a wealthy adult, Hetty favored plain oatmeal, even though by that time she could have afforded oysters Rockefeller and Delmonico steaks at every meal.)

At fifteen, she was enrolled in Mrs. Lowell's private school in Boston but felt constricted by the rules, daily routine and her inability to make friends. Counting her pennies continued to be a way of life. When her father suggested she invest what she had banked, she followed his advice. When she was little more than twenty, she decided to move to Manhattan. Living in the city, she continued to watch her bottom line. Her father gifted her $1,200 for a new wardrobe. Hetty spent $200 and put the rest in savings.

At twenty-one, Hetty inherited $7.5 million, a gigantic sum today. She'd been following the financial news since she was a child, reading aloud to her father and grandfather. It's no wonder she took to Wall Street and the intricacies of finance like a pig to a mudpie. Her fortunes grew. Growing up, she may not have been a well-rounded student—her spelling and writing were filled with mistakes—but when it came to math and finances, she was a whiz, constantly keeping a mental tab on every aspect of her fortune. She did her homework, reading whatever she could find about a stock before buying. Following a formula of picking

Hetty Green, the "Witch of Wall Street."
Courtesy the Library of Congress.

low-risk investments, careful scrutiny of tax laws and her normal penchant squeezing a dollar, she made a bundle. She wasn't shy about sharing her technique, saying, "I buy when things are low and nobody wants them. I keep them until they go up and people are anxious to buy."

Hetty's early thirties were disruptive. Her beloved aunt, Sylvia Ann, passed away, leaving her a fraction of the inheritance she expected. When Hetty learned that the will decreed that the bulk of her aunt's fortune would go to servants and charity, she challenged it, insisting that there was a previous will that left her all her aunt's worldly goods and assets and also nullified future wills. When she presented it to the court, they took it for a forgery. She lost the case.

Hetty was no social butterfly. For one thing, she could never tell whether people who were kind to her liked her for herself or for her money. Suitors were few and far between. How could she be sure whether a romantic interest was after her or her huge fortune?

Finally, cupid's arrow struck. Edward Henry Green was tall, imposing and handsome. Best of all, he had his own money that came from trading in silk, tobacco and tea. He and Hetty married on July 11, 1867, and had two children, Edward (Ned) and Sylvia. An announcement of Ned's birth in the *New Bedford Standard* noted, "Both millionaire and million-heir are doing well."

In 1878, Edward brought Hetty and the children to his home in Bellows Falls, a beautiful mansion at the corner of Westminster and Church Streets overlooking the Connecticut River. The home was built in 1806 by a Bellows Falls businessman, Captain William Hall, and had been purchased by Edward's grandfather Nathaniel Tucker.

Once in Vermont, Hetty's reputation as a miser grew. She was fond of sweets and bought broken cookies in bulk. She recycled berry boxes for the refund, and when visiting the grocer, she always demanded a free bone for her dog.

Children in Bellows Falls were spooked by Hetty. Hurrying down the streets of town in her perennial black dress, cape and hat, she looked like a witch from a picture book. It was said that she had only one outfit, and when the bottom of her black skirts grew gritty from dragging in the dust and mud, she would visit a laundry on the town square, telling them to wash only the bottom while she waited, unashamed, in her petticoats.

As much as Edward Green enjoyed his home in Vermont, he spent a good deal of time away. By most accounts, he and Hetty led independent lives. Even so, banks of the day had their own opinions about marriage and shared wealth. When Edward, not half as good with money as Hetty (or anywhere near as rich) ran short of funds, the banks would extend *her* cash flow to him, something she made sure to nip in the bud.

I can't say I blame Edward for distancing himself. Life with Hetty wasn't easy, especially for Ned and Sylvia. Some mothers love spoiling their children with fancy things, but not Hetty Green. Her kids wore hand-me-downs and suffered through the plainest of meals, even though their mother was worth millions of dollars. By many accounts, Hetty's dog received much better treatment.

When son Ned was a teenager, he was the victim of a collision with a child's Express wagon pulled by a Saint Bernard dog. (He might have been able to get out of the way if he didn't already have a lame leg thanks to an earlier childhood injury.) His leg was mangled and in desperate need of medical attention, so Hetty took him to the local free clinic, where she was immediately recognized. When the doctor, knowing full well her ability to pay, demanded she do so, Hetty left, convinced that with the help of some inexpensive home remedies the leg would heal by itself. Instead, it only got worse. Favoring the painful leg on a visit to his father, Ned fell down a flight of stairs. Edward called the doctor, who told him the leg would have to be amputated. He paid for the surgery.

Sylvia, born Harriet Sylvia Ann Howland Green in London on January 7, 1871, was a plain child and shown few favors by her mother. When they traveled, she slept in the same modest room, mere feet from Hetty. Like her mother, she had few friends. She eventually married wealthy Matthew Astor Wilkes, grandson of famed fur trader John Jacob Astor, when she was thirty-two and he was sixty-three. Hetty gave the two a proper wedding, but although her son-in-law was a millionaire in his own right, she still made him sign a prenup.

Hetty was plenty worried where Ned's romantic relationships were concerned. His first sexual experience was with a Chicago prostitute named

Hetty Green's outfit rarely varied. *Courtesy the Library of Congress.*

Mabel Harlow. His mother, thinking that he might let a gold digger run off with her fortune, made him promise not to marry, a promise he kept until after she died. Then, he married Mabel, but being his mother's son after all, he arranged a prenuptial agreement providing payments of $1,500 per month. Constantly seeking female attention, even after tying the knot, he boosted the finances of a string of young women whom he passed off as assistants or private secretaries, furnishing them with trust funds and tuition payments.

The press, endlessly fascinated by America's most famous miser, followed Hetty constantly. Of the attention she said, "My life is written for me down in Wall Street by people who, I assume, do not care to know one iota of the real Hetty Green. I am in earnest; therefore they picture me as heartless. I go my own way. I take no partner, risk nobody else's fortune, therefore I am Madame Ishmael, set against every man."

Stingy as she was, I wonder what the city of New York would have done without her?

A man named Russell Sage, nicknamed the "Money King," was, financially speaking, Hetty's male counterpart. Sage grew up poor in Verona, New York, and he made his money the old-fashioned way: he earned it. He attended public school, working as a farmhand until he was fifteen and then as an errand boy in his brother's grocery store.

He bought interest in a retail grocery and wholesale store, and he saved and saved some more. With his coffers full, but never as full as he liked, he began lending money and was charged at one point of usury, lending money at unreasonably high rates of interest. He was fined $500 and given a suspended sentence. Eventually, he bought a seat on the New York Stock Exchange. As stingy as Hetty, he was known to haggle with street vendors over the price of an apple. Legend has it that he withheld ten cents from an office boy's salary because the young man brought him an overpriced sandwich, costing fifteen cents instead of five.

In 1906, Russell Sage died. Enter Hetty, who believed in the power of cash and kept $20 million to $40 million on hand for emergencies. During the Panic of 1907, she, not Sage, wrote the city a check for $1.1 million and got a hefty return on her investment.

Hetty worked daily until her mid-seventies. Even in old age, she purchased little in the way of creature comforts. Everything she did was geared toward amassing a larger and larger fortune. After her husband Edward's death in 1902, Hetty moved to Hoboken, New Jersey, but her last years were spent in New York. She attributed her good health and long life to her habit of chewing baked onions, which must have been cheap in those days.

Hetty Green, the Witch of Wall Street, died on July 3, 1916, with an estate was estimated to be nearly $200 million. Of course, the woman who would rarely tip (and, when she did, no more than a nickel) kept her fortune in the family, leaving everything to Ned and Sylvia. Sylvia eventually gave the Green family home in Bellows Falls to the town. Neglected, it was demolished in 1940.

PSYCHO KILLER

When I'm not writing books, I'm taking people on haunted tours in Burlington, Vermont, with my company Queen City Ghostwalk. Many of my out-of-town guests are surprised to learn that back in the 1800s, there was a person living in Vermont's Queen City whose name and reputation is at least a little familiar to them. I'm talking about H.H. Holmes, "America's First Serial Killer."

In 1878, a fresh-faced Holmes had just changed his name from Herman Webster Mudgett. He was on track to become a doctor, living in Burlington and attending classes at Pomeroy Hall, the old medical school at the University of Vermont.

Most of what we know of Holmes's childhood is his own account, written in prison—some say to soften the public to his crimes. He was born in Gilmanton, New Hampshire, on May 16, 1860, to Levi and Theodate Mudgett. He couldn't point to much in his upbringing to account for his being a sociopath. His father was a "spare the rod, spoil the child" kind of guy, but so were a lot of dads in those days. He did recall that when he was in grammar school, some local bullies who knew his fear of the mysteries inside the office of a local doctor decided to have some fun with him by dragging him into the place and pushing him up against a skeleton. Their deed had the opposite effect from what was intended. Instead of being repelled, the young Holmes was fascinated. As a teen, he moved closer to what he thought would be a career in medicine, doing some apprentice work with Dr. Nahum Wight, who was a noted advocate of human dissection.

H.H. Holmes. *Courtesy the Library of Congress.*

I was shocked to learn that after graduating from high school at the age of sixteen, Holmes actually *taught* school for a while, first in Gilmanton, later in nearby Alton, New Hampshire, and finally in Mooers, New York. Apparently, the charming young man made a sensational first impression, and town after town hired him to form young minds at their local schoolhouses.

While in Alton, he met a woman named Clara Lovering. At eighteen, he married her but flew the coop, leaving her with his infant son to raise. (She was lucky, I suppose—at least he didn't kill her.) A later wife would tell authorities that Holmes adored children and wouldn't harm a hair on their heads. Nothing could be further from the truth.

He didn't take to teaching the way his employers took to him, and in most cases, after securing a position, he didn't stay long. When he left his job in Mooers, he traveled to Massachusetts and returned with a small boy who was only six or seven. Shortly afterward, the boy disappeared. When folks in Mooers asked where he was, Holmes told them he had "gone home." It was later believed that the boy was one of the madman's earliest victims.

During Holmes's stint at UVM, the pursuit of medical science meant the use of cadavers, and grave robbing was a popular pastime for stouthearted individuals hoping to make a quick buck. In those days, you could get a freshly dug cadaver for about thirty dollars—the same price you'd pay for a decent cow. I've got no proof, but I'm willing to bet that Holmes was happy to supply a cadaver for a fellow student without the messy, backbreaking, grave-digging part.

He left the medical school at UVM after just a year, ending up at the University of Michigan. He said that the school in Burlington was too small to suit his needs. I think the depraved little fish needed a bigger pond to draw from, Burlington being too small and too tightly knit a community to hide some of the things he was already up to.

At the University of Michigan, Holmes ran some of his very first insurance scams, stealing a number of cadavers from the anatomy lab, disfiguring them and then attributing to them the policies of fictitious individuals, saying they

The Holmes Murder Castle. *Courtesy the* Chicago Tribune.

had died in accidents, so he could claim the cash. This practice was known as a "Dead Man's Shuffle."

In 1892, after swindling an elderly couple out of their pharmacy business, Holmes built the infamous World's Fair Hotel, his Chicago "Murder Castle." He did this using several different construction crews so that, quite literally, one hand didn't know what the other hand was doing. He'd hire a contractor to complete a section and then fire the crew, claiming that they were incompetent. In this manner he was able to cut costs—and, oh yes, include rooms where guests would be asphyxiated or gassed to death, the evidence of their murders destroyed by a vat of acid and a small cremation device Homes had installed in the hotel's basement.

In 1894, Holmes was working his insurance scams with an associate named Benjamin Pitezel. He took out a policy on the man for $10,000, assuring him he would find a body, disfigure it and report the accidental death to the insurance company, after which they would split the payoff. Instead, he got Pitezel drunk and murdered him.

There was still the issue of collecting the insurance. Benjamin's wife, Carrie Pitezel, knew about the plan, but Holmes couldn't risk her identifying the body. She would know absolutely that the man he had killed was her husband. Instead, Holmes brought Pitezel's daughter, Alice, just fifteen years old, to identify the body. The girl wrote to her mother about her visit to the morgue, not the first mail she'd sent since traveling with Holmes. Carrie never got the letters because he intercepted every one, keeping them in a tin box. Later on, these letters would become crucial evidence.

After collecting the insurance money, Holmes convinced Carrie that in order for them to meet up with Ben Pitezel, whom she believed was still alive, they must travel separately. He offered to take Alice and two of the younger Pitezel children, Nellie and Howard, ages eleven and eight, with him. Both Carrie and Holmes were traveling, with Carrie removed from her offspring even though sometimes, unbeknownst to her, they were living in the same city. She went on this way for a while, going from pillar to post, believing that her husband and her children were still very much alive until finally Holmes, using the surname Judson, secured a living arrangement for her and her remaining children in Burlington, a place he knew well. He rented a duplex apartment at 26 North Winooski Avenue in a building owned by Mrs. T.G. Richardson and told Carrie she would go by the alias "Mrs. A.E. Cook." (The house still stands, just north of the best dive bar in Burlington, the Other Place. Never let it be said that beer and horror don't mix. And don't think I'm looking down my nose at the establishment by calling it a "dive bar." It's a local institution, open since 1980, on the former site of a bar that was named for one of our presidents, Millard Fillmore.)

After getting Carrie all settled in, Holmes rented a room at the Hotel Burlington, a fine establishment that once existed on St. Paul Street, next door to what is now the American Flatbread restaurant, a place known for its popular pizza made with local ingredients.

He had a plan to get rid of the remaining Pitezels, so he went slithering out to the nearest drugstore to pick up a quantity of nitroglycerin. He tucked it away in the basement of Carrie's new digs. He hoped she'd blow the place to high heaven, but that didn't happen.

Instead, in November 1894, Holmes was picked up in Boston on fraud charges, and when authorities met with Carrie, she filled in many of the blanks in Holmes's escapades and a devious trail of murder discovered by agent Frank Geyer.

Geyer, whose wife and daughter were killed in a fire a short time before he started investigating the Holmes case, followed Holmes's exploits through the United States and Canada, from Cincinnati to Indianapolis, Detroit and, eventually, Toronto. There he discovered the bodies of the two missing

Left: Carrie Pitezel. *Courtesy findagrave.com. Right*: Ben Pitezel. *Courtesy the* Chicago Tribune.

Pitezel girls and, soon after, in Indianapolis, the remains of their brother, young Howard.

On July 19, 1895, the Chicago police were finally able to enter the Murder Castle, and the place turned out to be "Body Part Central." They found a rib bone; a length of long, charred hair; a decomposed skull; and a pile of human skeleton parts mixed with animal bones, as though Holmes wanted the remains to look like garbage left over from the dog's breakfast. In addition to tattered clothing and nooses caked with blood, there was the stove in Holmes's office large enough to hold a human body.

In an excerpt from the *Chicago Tribune*'s article "'Modern Bluebeard': H.H. Holmes' Castle Reveals His True Character," the place was described for shocked and thrilled subscribers:

> *WHAT THE CASTLE IS LIKE*
> *But his castle, it now seems, as its labyrinths are explored, was his principal place of operation, and there it was that he planned and schemed and where many beautiful women are believed to have met their end. With such a place at his disposal, containing hundreds of rooms, torturous passages, secret chambers, trap-doors, dumbwaiters, with a rope for lowering down bodies into vats, a tank and a retort for disposing of them, it is hard to understand why he went elsewhere to commit murders.*
>
> *Holmes himself had planned the building, having no architect, and he took good care that the workmen were changed frequently, so that no one should know what the interior of the structure was like. He had air-tight*

chambers and a room of steel, lined with asbestos, where the wildest shrieks of his victims would be deadened, and he had a multitude of secret stairways and passages through which he could effect his escape at any time.

Depending on what you read or whom you talk to, Holmes killed either nine people or twenty-seven or more than two hundred. There's even some speculation that he jumped "across the pond" for a bit, ending up in London, where he made a reputation as Jack the Ripper, a fiend who in 1888, in just over a month's time, mutilated and killed five prostitutes in the Whitechapel District in the city's East End. As I write this, Holmes' great-great-grandson, Jeff Mudgett—who believes, based on a series of the murderer's diary entries, that Holmes was the Ripper—is caught up in efforts that might help him prove that his ancestor committed the Whitechapel murders.

Whether the mastermind murdered at home or abroad, I'm betting Holmes's death toll did number over two hundred. Why? I'm doing the math: All those rooms in his hotel and all those people in the White City. The fact that during the period of the Chicago World's Fair alone he was buying up chloroform like it was going out of style—bottles and bottles every week. Remember, he liked his hotel guests better when they were unconscious. And he made good money playing his Dead Man's Shuffle.

Holmes was tried in Philadelphia in the fall of 1895, just before Halloween. To say it was one of the most sensational and gossiped-about trials in memory would be an understatement. Grisly confessions of torture and murder have a way of selling newspapers, and the public was already hooked on Holmes due to the heavy coverage during his incarceration. In his confession, Holmes claimed, "I was born with the devil in me. I could not help the fact that I was a murderer, no more than the poet can help the inspiration to sing."

He was found guilty and finally executed on May 7, 1896, just nine days before his thirty-sixth birthday. He was offered religious counsel and refused to confess his sins. His was a death by hanging that took longer than most. After the trap was sprung, his heart continued to beat for five minutes.

If a guest on my haunted tour isn't terribly knowledgeable about Holmes, they usually ask me after the walk if they can still visit the Murder Castle on a trip to Chicago. The answer, both fortunate and unfortunate, is no. When the police investigation of Holmes's World's Fair Hotel was concluded, the building was purchased by one A.M. Clark, who intended to capitalize on the public's fascination with the horrific things that happen there. He never got the chance. On August 19, 1895, the building caught fire, and an explosion

Holmes made the headlines. *Courtesy the* Chicago Evening Star.

shattered the first-floor windows. The roof collapsed, and the upper floors of the building were destroyed. The first floor was rebuilt and housed service and retail space until the complex was sold in 1937. In 1938, the property was sold and the building demolished. A United States Post Office was built on the site. It is rumored to be very, very, haunted.

TRUE DETECTIVE STORIES

$\mathcal{P}$hilosopher Henry David Thoreau said, "An early morning walk is a blessing for the whole day." Such was not the case for eighteen-year-old Harold Jackson, a visitor to Barre, Vermont, who on the morning of May 4, 1919, left his hotel at about 7:30 a.m. and stumbled upon something gruesome in a flower garden on Main Street, just feet from the town square: the body of Lucina Courser Broadwell, a young wife and mother who also lived in the community. Jackson found her facedown, wearing only shoes, stockings and a pair of kid gloves. Her clothing and underpinnings, some of them torn, had been stuffed under her body and thrown in a heap nearby.

Jackson went to the police station to report what he had found, but there was nobody there. He doubled back, and at the electric company, he came upon Officer A.B. Curtis, who doubted the teen's story but followed him back to the scene anyway. Shocked, Curtis placed a coat over the deceased and then went to alert the state's attorney. Investigators arrived and combed the area, and evidentiary photos were taken. It was noted that Lucina's legs were crossed, and her gloves were pulled down away from her wrists. Pictures showed the woman's belongings scattered varying distances from her corpse, as though someone playing a diabolical game of Hansel and Gretel had dropped them one by one. Her hat was lying three feet away. Her gold watch, etched with her initials and still ticking, was thirteen feet away. Her empty purse was five feet beyond that. There was a man's white handkerchief around her neck, and her hands were tied with a piece of

Lucina Broadwell. *Courtesy the Barre Times-Argus.*

fabric torn from her "unmentionables." It was obvious that the poor thing had been strangled.

Based on what they found, investigators believed that she was bound and gagged sometime before her body was deposited on Main Street. On the evening of her death, Lucina Broadwell had told her husband she was going to a picture show. What really happened the night of the barbaric killing of the twenty-nine year-old mother of three, on the cusp of that summer of 1919, made for unsavory entertainment that kept the nearly seventeen thousand residents of Barre and the rest of the state gossiping throughout the fall.

Who would want to kill Lucina Broadwell? It was shocking and baffling, to say the least. Born in Johnson, Vermont, on July 26, 1889, she had been married for nine years to Harry Broadwell, who made his living as a carpenter. She was a petite woman, a little over five feet tall and weighing about 105 pounds. She had dark, arresting eyes and prominent cheekbones. She kept house and cared for her children, Doris, Hildred and Wendell. Her daily life seemed unremarkable.

On May 7, the day of Lucina's funeral, a detective arrived from Massachusetts. James Rodney Wood headed up his own agency in Boston. The strong-jawed, steely-eyed PI was considered the best detective in New England. In fact, his exploits had been featured in *True Detective Stories from New England*, real-life accounts that titillated readers of the *Boston Evening American* and the *Boston Sunday Advertiser*. He'd been hired by the state to conduct a full investigation into the murder.

He and his team met with Vermont attorney general Frank C. Archibald and local authorities to be briefed on the details of the case. Evidence collected by the local police department pointed to Lucina having been murdered at the Buzell Hotel and then moved to the garden, where she was found by Mr. Jackson. Investigators believed they already had a suspect: the victim's husband, Harry Broadwell. Broadwell had *also* been out the evening of the May 3, and it was common knowledge that he and Lucina had a contentious, possibly violent, relationship.

Before he talked to the suspect, Wood wanted time to familiarize himself with the crime scene, but he wanted to do it alone. He spent his entire first night in Vermont looking for evidence in secret. He went to the lot where Lucina was found. He walked to the nearby Buzell Hotel, studying lighting conditions. He got back to his room shortly before breakfast, convinced that Lucina wasn't killed at the Buzell Hotel. He was ready to question Harry Broadwell to learn his whereabouts on the night his wife was murdered.

After interviewing Lucina's husband and checking his alibi, Wood was convinced that he couldn't be the murderer. Broadwell had spent the bulk of the evening with a woman named Eva Dow. He had more than one witness who could attest to his movements that night. He did admit to roughing up his spouse on occasion, and he mentioned there *had* been an incident involving him pulling a knife on her because she'd called him a liar. She'd called the police that time. But, he said, they had not argued the day she died. Wood did learn something else he found interesting: Broadwell made it clear that his wife of less than a decade tended to be "sporty" and that he had reason to believe she had been having an affair. He said he knew it to be with someone who lived at Belle Parker's place.

Isabelle "Belle" Parker had a house at 110 South Main Street. She kept quarters upstairs and rented rooms downstairs. It was well known by those who were into that sort of thing that Belle was running a brothel and hosting "cheating" parties at her place. Harry had also told Wood that his wife had a good friend, Grace Grimes, who had left Barre and moved to the Boston area. Maybe she had told Grace something about her whereabouts the night of the murder.

It didn't take long for Wood's office to contact Grimes. She explained that she and Lucina wrote each other regularly and that Lucina had, in a letter sent on the day of her murder, confided she'd met about a lodger of Belle's named George. Grace knew about the so-called cheating parties because when Lucina had written, she mentioned she had participated in them on several occasions.

Grimes's information checked out. George R. Long, who was employed by a nearby garage, was a tenant at Belle's house. When questioned, he denied knowing Lucina.

Soon after, Isabelle Parker was questioned and her "party" house searched. During the search, Wood found Isabelle's diary, filled with names, addresses and telephone numbers of her "guests." Belle's customers would have reason to be concerned about her "little red book." She didn't think to use pseudonyms, and many of them were among the most prominent and

Main Street, Montpelier, early 1900s. *Courtesy the University of Vermont.*

well-to-do folks in Barre. The pages of the book offered equal-opportunity scandal, since both men and women patronized her house of ill repute.

Belle came clean to Wood about the secret to her success. She would go about Barre with an ear toward finding men and women were who were inclined to be "sporty"—as we might put it in modern terms, "looking for some action." If she heard a married man liked to have his cake and eat it, too, she'd get to know him and his inclinations and then let him know that a woman she knew was interested in him and desired a meeting. She'd arrange a time for both to come to her place for an introduction, and if they hit it off, it was party time. Belle profited because the gentleman of the two would pay her out of his pocket for the use of a room. Belle told Wood that Lucina had been at her place the evening of May 3 and that she believed George Long and the victim had had dinner together.

A week after Lucina's body was found, Wood, bolstered by new information, questioned Long again. This time, Long admitted knowing the woman but insisted he hadn't killed her. He said he'd gotten out of work at about eight o'clock, had a meal with Mrs. Parker and went to bed at about ten o'clock. He said he remembered a short while after he'd been asleep that he heard noises, a conversation coming from the front room. He claimed that, thinking nothing of it, he went back to sleep. He said when he woke at 5:00 or 5:30 a.m. the next morning that Belle was already up and talking to a man from Montpelier—either a Spaniard or an Italian, Long wasn't sure which.

Sometime later, Long was questioned again. This time his story was different, with new characters. A woman from Graniteville whose name he didn't know had been at the house. A man named Joe Johnson, and some other guy named Oscar something—he couldn't recall his last name—had been there as well.

It all sounded sketchy, to say the least, and Long had no idea, while he was racking up falsehoods, how the circumstantial evidence was stacking up against him. Wood had been gathering information that would prove invaluable to the prosecution in the case. The night he'd gone on his solo investigation of the crime scene, he'd found a tire track beside the curb where Lucina's body was dumped. He was able to trace it back to a car rented by none other than George Long. And there was another thing: the men's handkerchief that was twisted around Lucina's neck had been given to Long by a man named Eddie Barron.

On May 15, George Long and Isabelle Parker were arrested and taken to the Washington County Jail. A little digging revealed that George Long was living in Montpelier under an assumed name. His real name was George Rath. It was a moniker attached to an impressively long rap sheet. He had lived, previously, at the Buzzell Hotel; then a friend had told him about Belle's place. He became a regular. Then he moved in.

Long's trial began on October 7, 1919. It was a packed house. Prosecutors had not just the strong circumstantial evidence provided by Wood's

Belle Parker's place. *Courtesy Dave "Tuck" Tucker.*

investigation but also the various conflicting statements of George Long, including one in which he admitted paying Lucina for sex the night of the murder, with Mrs. Parker providing the room.

On October 24, the court heard testimony from a woman named Daisy Luce, who testified that she spoke with George Long the morning Lucina's body was discovered. During their conversation, Long had told her that "there would be one less woman in Barre" that day.

Long's trial lasted one month before it went to the jury. In its closing statement, the defense claimed that Long had no motive to kill Lucina since they were "intimate partners," but the jury, when it gave its verdict, came down on the side of the evidence provided by James Rodney Wood. On October 31, at 3:30 p.m., the jury found George Long guilty of second-degree murder. He was returned to prison pending his sentencing hearing on November 5. His punishment would be life at the Windsor State Prison. He appealed, but the Supreme Court found his crime "a brutal killing—one unmistakably indicating cool depravity of heart and wanton cruelty" and denied his appeal.

With Long locked away, it was Isabelle Parker's turn to face the music. While she had originally been charged as an accessory to murder, her charges were reduced to "conducting a house of ill fame." She pleaded guilty and was sentenced to two to four years in prison. Because her health was poor, she was allowed her freedom while she petitioned the governor for clemency, but her luck had run out. She was denied clemency and served two and a half years in prison. She died on September 5, 1922.

Census records indicate that Lucina's husband, the hot-tempered Harry Broadwell, moved with his children to Chittenden County. Wendell, Hildred and Doris all survived to adulthood. All three married. Harry died in South Burlington, Vermont, on November 5, 1954, at the age of sixty-four after what was described, in the Card of Thanks section of the *Burlington Free Press*, as a "short illness" He was buried in Plattsburgh, New York.

CUNNING RASCALITY

*I*t used to be that whenever someone I knew had a brush with the law, I would wonder what my felonious superpower might be if I ever turned to a life of crime. Then one day, my friend Sharon Meyer, a co-worker at Vermont's local CBS affiliate, WCAX-TV, left her bull mastiff alone in her car to run into the building for something she'd forgotten. The dog accidentally hit the gear shift and rolled the car into the middle of the company parking lot. No one was harmed, and we all had a good laugh when another co-worker asked whether the dog, whose name was Mouse (what else do you name a big, slobbering beast who was supposed to be the runt of the litter?), had a license to drive. I'd done some dog sitting for Sharon while she was on vacation and had taken some color photos of her four-legged friend. With a little creative writing, some unauthorized logos (sorry, Vermont DMV) and a laminating machine, I made a Vermont Operator's License for Mouse. Voila: a forger was born.

In June 1854, a small crime wave hit Rutland, Vermont, when a quartet of strangers came north from Philadelphia with a scheme to bilk the local bank out of a lot of dough. Matthew Matthews (described as "an old bejeweled sinner"), John Gill, Charles Sexton (the youngest of the bunch) and William Mintzer were well acquainted before they arrived in the Green Mountain State, but once they crossed state lines, no one would have known it.

In Rutland, working individually, the four began to make small deposits into accounts they'd opened at the Rutland, Vergennes and Farmers and Mechanics Banks. After that, each of the men would request certified checks.

Rutland Bank, 1904. *Courtesy the University of Vermont.*

Armed with felonious intent and the signatures of the cashiers at each bank, they put their fancy penmanship to work creating remarkable forgeries of each teller's John Henry. In two weeks' time, it was ready, set, counterfeit!

First they tested the Rutland Bank with a check drawn on Farmers and Mechanics in the amount of $800. When their efforts passed with flying colors, they waited a few days and floated a bigger check at the Rutland Bank, drawn on the Vergennes bank for $2,900. The supervisory cashier, Mr. Page, was trying to get some packages ready for express delivery and didn't catch the signature immediately, but *Burlington Free Press* noted that he possessed "all the qualities of a superior cashier" and wrote that "only the most adroit and practiced villains could have escaped his notice." They did, but not for long.

Twelve hours later, the big "uh-oh" was discovered by Mr. Page, and the police were alerted. Their luck had run out, and the criminal cronies fled. Within three days, Matthews (alias Jim Morton) and Gill (alias Samuel Becroft) were caught up with in Montreal. Mintzer and Sexton were arrested in Philadelphia. Matthews and Gill confessed their act of

"Cunning Rascality," as the *Free Press* headline declared it, and were in due time thrown in the pokey in their respective cities of capture. Most of the money was recovered.

A requisition from the governor of Vermont, Stephen Royce, brought them back to face the music. At the trial, although $1,000 was found on Mintzer, he turned state's evidence against the other three, who were convicted of forgery and false pretenses. "Cunning rascality" indeed.

As a final note, I worry that the declining interest in teaching handwriting in school will mean underachievers like me will have nothing easy to fall back on to boost their grammar school grade point average. Picture me mourning the slow death of the "Palmer Method." Developed by Austin Palmer in the late 1800s, this basis for good handwriting that's been used for more than one hundred years was designed to be simpler and easier than the old way of writing, the "Spencerian Method," which had been in use since the 1840s.

I'm sure the handwriting tutorial employed by the forgers in this chapter predates even the "Spencerian Method," and I can't help think that with Palmer they would have been *much* better off. Why? Proponents of the writing style said it was faster than the old method and would allow people to better compete with a typewriter, but in this case, what might have been helpful was how educators believed the regimentation provided by practicing the method would be useful to foster discipline, build character and even reform delinquents.

MERRY MARY ROGERS

*A*ccording to statistics published in the spring of 2017, there were 1,456 prisoners executed in the United States since the U.S. Supreme Court reinstated the death penalty in 1976. Only 16 of them were women.

Historically, execution of female offenders has been rare, making up only 3.6 percent of the 15,931 confirmed executions in the United States and its colonies since around 1608. It's not hard to see why that when Mary Rogers went to the gallows for murder in Windsor, Vermont, back in 1905, it shocked an entire nation.

Mary Rogers grew up in Hoosick Falls, New York, the daughter Charles and Johanna Bennett. She was attractive, with large, dark eyes, jet-black hair and a creamy complexion, but in spite of her good looks, she wasn't popular. Schoolmates took to calling her the "Mope." Their taunts made her grow wild and unpredictable, easily excitable and impulsive, and then suddenly plunged into gloom once again. In court testimony, witnesses said she was a poor student, "weak mentally," and it was revealed that she was once committed to the Hudson State Hospital, a home for the mentally insane in Poughkeepsie, New York. A maternal uncle, Patrick Dwyer, had also been committed to the asylum. (In court, Mary's mother claimed that her brother was not insane but had improved and been released. His diagnosis was "extreme melancholia.")

But Mary Rogers had more than one reason to feel a little off-kilter. Her parents were both heavy drinkers, and to say her home life was chaotic would be an understatement. Her father, whom a witness at her trial called "a moral degenerate," abused her physically and emotionally and tried to kill her on more than on occasion, including on the very day she was born.

When she was fifteen, a change of scenery for Mary arrived in the person of Marcus Rogers, a Hoosick Falls farmworker more than ten years her senior. He was attracted to her despite her unconventional behavior, and in 1898, they married and moved to Shaftsbury, Vermont.

Once married, Mary didn't magically turn placid and matronly. In fact, she gained a reputation for coloring outside the lines of her marriage vows. A few years after she wed Marcus Rogers, she became pregnant, delivering a healthy baby boy in 1901. He didn't live long enough for her to get the hang of mothering. Upon hearing her explanation that she accidentally dropped her precious bundle and he hit his head, people who knew her well were convinced she'd killed the infant intentionally.

Money was a constant bone of contention for the couple, and Marcus grew tired of trying to make ends meet in Shaftsbury. He decided to move back to Hoosick Falls to work on his brother's farm. Mary declined to go with him, choosing instead to stay on in Vermont alone. Sort of.

Mary, in her husband's absence, really got around. She dated a man named Morris Knapp and also dallied with two brothers named Levi and Leon Perham. She was particularly keen on Morris, whose family was respected in town and quite well off. Their extracurricular activities turned to the idea of marriage. But Mary was already hitched. What was a girl to do?

In a fairly nervy move, she asked her sometime love interest Levi Perham to help her bump off her husband. Levi had the good sense to say no. But his younger brother, Leon, with his still biologically immature "teen brain," agreed to help her with the deed.

Mary, pretending an ongoing interest in her husband and their relationship, asked him to come to Bennington for a visit. On August 9, 1902, he met her at a picnic grounds near the Walloomsac River. Little did he know that Leon was hiding nearby. The husband and wife spent a while catching up, with Marcus telling Mary he was discouraged by talk he'd heard about her sexual liaisons with other men. Mary made the claims out to be jealous gossip. She stroked his hair and then animatedly told him of the exciting thing a friend of hers had seen at the Rutland Opera House. Houdini had been performing and had done the most marvelous rope tricks. Would he let her show him one her friend had described? Marcus agreed.

As soon as his hands were tied behind his back, Mary held a handkerchief doused with chloroform over his face, and Leon, who had jumped out of the bushes, helped. By the time they were finished with Mary's unsuspecting mate, his face was bruised, his ear torn nearly off and his skull crushed. Mary removed an envelope from her husband's coat. Inside it was an insurance policy she knew he always carried. She then attached a "suicide" note she had prepared to a man's hat, which she tied to a nearby tree. The note read, "Blame no one, as I have at last put an end to my miserable life, as my wife knows I have threatened it…everyone knows I have not anything or nobody to live for, and so blame no one as my last request, Marcus Rogers. Mary Rogers, I hope you will be happy."

Soon after the murder, Mary began trying to collect Marcus's insurance payout, applying for it even before his body had been autopsied. Thanks to inconsistencies in her story, the authorities were keeping a watchful eye on Mary and questioning her associates. It didn't take long for young Leon Perham to buckle. At an inquest, he broke down and told authorities everything, with no plea deal. Prosecutors, feeling sorry for the seventeen-year-old and not terribly quick-witted suitor, saw to it he received a sentence of life in prison as punishment for his role in Marcus Rogers's murder. A *Burlington Free Press* reporter, apparently outraged, responded this way to Perham's lucky break: "The finger that has pointed accusingly at the daughters of Eve for countless ages may well falter in the face of this yielding, murdering, conniving, betraying, cowardly thing, permitted, for some inscrutable reason, to wear the likeness of a man."

The prosecution painted Mary a harlot, an adulteress and a cold, unwomanly monster. It was noted that when her mother visited her in prison, asking if she should send a priest to hear her confession, she replied, "You can take your priest and go to hell. I have no use for one." Admittedly she wasn't doing much for her own PR.

On December 22, 1903, she was found guilty and sentenced to death by hanging, but nobody, not even Mary, thought she would really hang. Before the Rogers case, there was only one woman who had been legally hanged in Vermont: Emeline Meaker, who in 1883, while foster mother to her husband's niece, poisoned the girl with strychnine. For more than a decade, the legislature had commuted every death sentence that was handed down, and Mary Rogers was only nineteen. Unfortunately, it chose her case to set an example and voted not to commute her sentence.

There was a huge public outcry. The idea of punishing a woman—a mentally incompetent woman, some believed—didn't sit well. The case

Left to right: Marcus Rogers, Mary Rogers and Leon Perham. *Courtesy New England Historical Society.*

was appealed. Vermont governor Charles Bell received more than forty thousand letters from around the country asking him to spare Mary's life. In Connecticut, Mrs. William J. Blickensderfer, sympathetic to Mary's cause, had been paying lawyers for her appeal and was calling on the women of America to rally around her cause. In Cincinnati alone, petitioners gathered thirty thousand signatures, asking that Mary Rogers be shown mercy.

Locked up in prison in Windsor, Mary received thousands of letters. People sent gifts of food and candy. Still viewed as mentally unstable and now somewhat of a celebrity, the young woman was far from contrite. Conspiring with a prison matron, Mary was able to have sexual relations with a convicted rapist and a prison guard. When questioned, the matron claimed that Mary had put her under a spell. Mary was placed in solitary confinement. It was feared that she was attempting to become pregnant to sway public opinion. Part of her plan worked. She gave birth to the nearly full-term child, delivered stillborn.

On November 27, 1905, Governor Bell signed her death warrant and set the date of her execution for December 8, 1905, even though he had received more than seven thousand letters calling for a reprieve, sent by people from all walks of life. Some thought the governor was drawing a hard line because of growing public opinion that the death penalty in Vermont was joke. An article in the *San Francisco Call* said as much:

San Francisco Call, Volume 97, Number 61, 30 January 19
MARY ROGERS READY TO DIE
For the First Time Condemned Woman Appears Resigned to Her Fate
SENDS FOR CLERGYMAN
Attorney Attributes to Public Clamor the Verdict that Sends Her to the Gallows
Special Dispatch to the Call.

WINDSOR, *Vt., Jan. 29.—"Christ, looking beneath the exterior animal and seeing the life in the deepest recesses of the soul, sought it not to destroy," was the theme of Rev. Jonathan K. Fuller's impressive discourse to 170 prisoners in the State prison chapel this morning.*

"No man or woman is so depraved but we can see beneath the animal, after all its rioting is over, that within every soul which, if turned aright, may bring every man or woman into the glory of the Redeemer."

While no direct reference was made to Mary Mabel Rogers, who is to be hanged on Friday for the murder of her husband, Marcus Rogers, there was no mistaking the chaplain's meaning.

After the service the pastor went to the cell and spent two hours with Mary Rogers, who knelt in prayer beside him. To-day, for the first time, she signified to Superintendent Oaks that she desired that Chaplain Fuller should be at her execution. The chaplain will administer communion on Thursday or Friday morning, before the final scene on the scaffold.

For the first two nights after her transfer to the condemned cell, Mary Rogers never closed her eyes. Since then she has become more resigned, but does not sleep well and passes many wakeful hours in the night. "I have not been guilty of all they have accused me of," she said, "but I have been a very wicked woman." Her concern seems to be more for the wanton life she has led and her future than for the murder for which her life is demanded. She does not mention that now, nor has she alluded to it in weeks.

"Unfortunately for Mary Rogers," said a Windsor attorney to-day, "there was an outcry in the Vermont papers that the law prescribing death penalty had become a farce. The death penalty in the case of seven murderers, all sentenced to be hanged, had been commuted, and the demand was that somebody be hanged. Just then unhappy fate produced Mary Rogers as that person. That is why the Legislature was so insistent that no change in the law be made."

In Bradford, Vermont, Admiral Charles Edgar Clark, a hero of the Spanish-American War, was a very vocal opponent to the idea of executing Mary. His family, with his support, demanded that his portrait, which hung inside the Vermont Statehouse, be turned toward the wall in shame of such a barbarous act. Even the Windsor County sheriff, who would be called on to execute Mary, hired a lawyer to try to persuade the governor to grant clemency. He said that he would preside over the execution only under protest.

Still, no single public official or body with any say in the matter would move for clemency. Not the Vermont Supreme Court, the U.S. Supreme Court or even President Roosevelt, who had also

Governor Charles J. Bell would not commute Mary Rogers's sentence. *Courtesy State of Vermont Archives.*

received letters asking him to intervene. Emotions ran high. With no relief in sight, an anonymous benefactor offered a reward of $2,000 to anyone who could manage to slip a vial of poison past the prison staff so Mary could die peacefully.

The morning of the execution, Governor Bell met with Mary's lawyers one last time, but he was weary of the whole affair. The controversy over the woman's impending execution had made his recent trip to San Francisco a living hell. He was ready to wash his hands of her. His final word on the matter were, "I know of no law that is not as much for a woman as for a man."

On December 8, 1905, Mary set tongues inside the prison wagging one last time. Just before her execution, she intimated that she was again pregnant, by yet another inmate, but the execution went on as planned. Well, mostly as planned. Mary walked to the scaffold, took off her glasses and gave them to the sheriff. A hood was pulled over her head and the noose placed around her neck. When the trapdoor beneath her opened, it was discovered that the rope was either stretched or cut too long. Mary's feet hit the ground under the gallows. According to some witnesses, she was hauled back up by the sheriff. Her neck did not break. For fourteen excruciating minutes, bystanders waited while Mary Rogers strangled to death.

GYPSIES, TRAMPS AND THIEVES

*Y*ears ago, I heard a comedian say, "When people meet my family, they get the feeling that somewhere out there, there's a carnival running itself." I laughed because the line reminded me of my family. We're not career carnies by any stretch, but my grandmother did run away with the fair. Fortunately, she came back.

My point is that my family is a big bag of mixed nuts, and we're part French Canadian. That, and plenty of other characteristics attributable to our ancestors, would have made it hard for us to escape the notice of the Vermont Eugenics Survey.

When you think eugenics, you probably think Nazis. But Nazis weren't the only ones trying to improve the human population by controlled breeding. Thank Sir Francis Galton, a big egghead from England, who spent a great deal of time thinking about "selective parenthood" and coined not just the term *eugenics* but a phrase we still throw around today: "Nature versus nurture."

The practice of eugenics meant the creation of "favorable" people— people who were smart, heathy and good looking. To attain the goal of making everybody desirable, you had to get rid of the defective or subpar genes and traits found in certain parts of the population. If "bad heredity" was the root of the "decline in the quality of life in Vermont's hamlets and villages," well, then, it was time to nip that in the bud. The Vermont legislature heard testimony from doctors and scientific "experts" on the merits of weeding out the "unfit."

Sir Francis Galton. *Courtesy the Library of Congress.*

In Vermont, the Eugenics Record Office, which was founded in 1910, went on record as saying that officials "would comb the state…and after finding them [defectives], would act as an executive agent in bringing to the courts the defectives for disposition in institutions or sterilization."

The first sterilization law was passed by the legislature in 1912, and as you might expect, slanted research aimed for easy targets, like people who were already poor or victims of domestic dysfunction. For instance, a bulk of investigations delved into the backgrounds of "bad girls" in juvenile reformatories. The findings led the sitting head of state, Governor Mead, to write that the law should be applied "chiefly to those of the female sex" as a safeguard against those young girls with "loose morals" having children who had loose morals too.

The United States Army's Draft Board Exams administered to men drafted in 1917 showed that Vermont had the second-highest "defect rate" in the nation. It was wondered if poor genetics had contributed to the apparent "inefficiency" of inductees.

Around that time, the future kingpin of the eugenics scene in Vermont was waiting in the wings. He was a University of Vermont zoology professor named Henry F. Perkins. Perkins was the only son of George Henry Perkins, a professor of natural sciences and Dean of Arts and Sciences at the University of Vermont. His father's lily-white ancestors came over on the *Mayflower*. His mother was a philanthropist and the head of the Vermont chapter of the Woman's Christian Temperance Union. He had spent his childhood among the well-to-do of Burlington's Hill Section. After graduating with honors from UVM and getting his PhD in zoology from Johns Hopkins University, he came back to UVM to teach biology, entomology, anatomy, physiology and embryology.

In 1922, already a fan of the writings of Sir Francis Galton, Perkins began teaching courses in heredity and evolution. His heredity class was the seed that sprouted into the Vermont Eugenics Survey. He took a sabbatical to solicit funds and began the collection of data on Vermonters of various backgrounds and ethnicities.

The Vermont Eugenics Survey and, later, the Vermont Country Life Project were intended to eradicate "defectives." Who, exactly, were considered "defectives" under Perkins's survey? It was a long list. African Americans, Abenakis, illiterates, the illegitimate, the insane, gays (called "queer" for their purposes), the poor, the immoral, the dishonest, sex offenders, rapists, syphilitics, fibbers, travelers, epileptics, alcoholics, those with speech defects or poor memory, those deemed shiftless and many more.

Once the survey investigated "pedigrees of degeneracy" among Vermont's rural poor and identified those who were lacking, they came up with a few nifty solutions to the conundrum of how to keep anything less than the cream of the crop from tainting Vermont's gene pool: the state could invest

Henry F. Perkins. *Courtesy the Burlington Free Press.*

in institutions and, of course, sterilize, sterilize, sterilize.

Marriage restriction was also a recommended safeguard. Eugenics was a lesson to be careful who you loved. Even if you weren't deficient in some way—and not the one in danger of being institutionalized or sterilized—you could still be fined for marrying an "idiot." "Normal" couples were encouraged to go forth and multiply. The theory was that the genetically gifted could improve life for everyone if they would procreate generously, so the good stock in Vermont would overcome the bad.

In 1927, Perkins created a new rural survey that resulted in the Vermont Commission on Country Life. Along with it came a report, "Rural Vermont: A Program for the Future," which led to the investigation and documentation of entire families, with information about them collected and shared with Vermont state agencies and institutions and even with neighboring states. Reading the records is a real eye-opener. In them, public authorities like teachers and social workers clearly aim prejudices at a variety of ethnic and socioeconomic groups, like the Irish, Italians, French Canadians, Native Americans, black groups and the poor.

I have an aunt, a pretty sharp cookie, who happens to be French Canadian. She's told me stories of growing up back in the 1930s on a houseboat on Lake Champlain. Her family was poor, and she and her siblings would walk the railroad tracks to pick up coal the train cars dropped so they would have fuel to cook their food and warm their home. Families like hers would have been targeted by Perkins's study as a "pirate family" or "gypsies"—in other words, undesirable and defective.

Perkins wasn't the only high-profile individual responsible for lumping people in columns here in Vermont. Harriet Abbott was a graduate of Vassar College and the Chicago School of Civics and Philanthropy. She was hired by the Vermont Children's Aid Society as the first district agent out of Bellows Falls, Vermont. Harriet gained families' trust by telling them she was writing a book. She delved deep into their histories, wanting to know where their grandparents came from, the occupations of various family members,

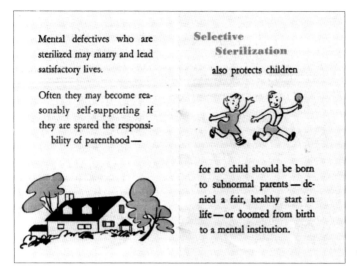

Mental defectives who are sterilized may marry and lead satisfactory lives.

Often they may become reasonably self-supporting if they are spared the responsibility of parenthood—

Selective Sterilization

also protects children

for no child should be born to subnormal parents — denied a fair, healthy start in life — or doomed from birth to a mental institution.

Eugenics propaganda. *Courtesy of North Carolina Office of Justice for Sterilization Victims.*

their level of education and so on. The families she targeted had gotten on her roster because they were deemed "primitive."

On March 31, 1931, the Vermont legislature passed "An Act for Human Betterment by Voluntary Sterilization." It resulted in a total of 253 sterilizations that year; two-thirds of them were performed on women, and 80 percent of those included in the survey were said to be "mentally deficient." It may have been part of the melting pot that was the United States, but in Vermont, immigrant culture was something to deride, not celebrate.

People did object. Irish and French Canadian communities, particularly, were vocal in their opposition to the eugenics survey, but politically connected and wealthier Protestant wonks won out over the vocal minority.

The Eugenics Survey closed in 1936, but eugenics education continued, as did the tracking of "problem" families and people considered unfit to conceive. Now, weeding out the "undesirables" fell to Department of Public Welfare and other government entities. Forced or coerced sterilization in Vermont continued into the 1970s, particularly among the western Abenaki tribes.

Whatever happened to Henry F. Perkins? It turns out that despite his devotion to genetic perfection, the old boy was afflicted with the urge to drink. He spent much of his life trying to weed it out of Vermont's gene pool when he should have been looking in his own backyard. He passed at the age of seventy-nine as a result of liver failure after spending years as a bedridden alcoholic.

DADDY AND PEACHES
AT THE EQUINOX HOTEL

The Equinox Hotel in Manchester is a Vermont landmark with a capital *V*.

Since the creation of the original wooden two-story structure in 1769, the place has been through lots of changes and has had many names: Marsh Tavern, Thaddeus Munson's New Inn, Widow Black's Inn, Vanderlip's Hotel, the Taconic, the Orvis Hotel and now the Equinox House, which opened its doors in 1853.

Mary Todd Lincoln loved the place, although her husband was too busy to visit. He was planning a trip to the Equinox before his assassination. Other high-profile guests have included Major General Abner Doubleday, who fired the first shot in defense of Fort Sumter in the opening battle of the Civil War; Ulysses S. Grant; William Howard Taft; Theodore Roosevelt; Benjamin Harrison; and Calvin Coolidge. Filmmaker Ken Burns and best-selling author Stephen King have been more modern guests of the Equinox.

None of the previous guests mentioned—even Mary Todd Lincoln, with her penchant for séances—have been quite as titillating as Edward "Daddy" Browning and his cuddle-bug "Peaches."

Edward West Browning was a multimillionaire whose first marriage at the age of forty-one to Adele Lowen, a woman eighteen years his junior, wasn't all wine and roses. They lived a life of pure luxury, but for Adele, it wasn't enough. She wanted a baby, so Edward advertised for one. Soon they had two: Marjorie and Dorothy.

But Adele discovered that motherhood wasn't all it was cracked up to be, and she started seeing her dentist—a *lot*. His name was Charles H. Wilen, and he was twenty-eight, charming and handsome. Stories indicate that Wilen had a great dentist chair–side manner and then some. He was, admittedly, a womanizer and told people that the "DDS" designation in front of his name stood for "Devilish Dental Sheik."

Patients with whom the "Sheik" was not amorously involved got annoyed waiting outside his office while he was busy examining Adele's, um, molars. And Edward wasn't too pleased, either, when the dental bills started coming in. As for Wilen, once Adele was in his emotional clutches, he began soaking her for expensive gifts. What did she get from him, aside from the excitement of an illicit affair? She got gonorrhea.

In 1923, she and Edward divorced, and she took Marjorie to live with her, leaving nine-year-old Dorothy with her ex. Edward moved with his daughter to a mansion on Long Island, but both of them felt that something was lacking. Edward hit the classifieds again:

> ADOPTION—*Pretty refined girl, about 14 years old, wanted by aristocratic family of large wealth and highest standing: will be brought up as own child among beautiful surroundings, with every desirable luxury, opportunity, education, travel, kindness, care, love.*

A girl named Mary Spas answered the ad, and it seemed that she was just what the doctor ordered. Her parents were keen on the idea, too, and in no time at all, Mary Spas was tooling around in Browning's peacock blue Rolls-Royce. Then, disaster: Edward found out that Mary Spas was not a teenager but rather an aspiring actress of twenty-one!

Browning, who loved the notoriety attached to being a wealthy guy, didn't seem to mind when his search for the right much-too-young-for-him girl had newspapers calling him the "Cinderella Man." More than 3 million women and young girls hoping to be "adopted" sent letters to him, offering themselves. He kept their proposals stored in a room he built just for that purpose. But the question remained: would he and Dorothy ever find the perfect playmate?

On March 5, 1926, at a hotel dance, their prayers—or Edward's, anyway—were answered in the form of Frances Belle Heenan. Heenan was just fifteen years old. At five-foot-six, she was round, firm and fully packed. As was only fitting, people called her "Peaches."

Peaches Browning. *Courtesy the Library of Congress.*

Peaches's mother, whose elevator must not have gone all the way to the top floor, encouraged her daughter's relationship with the by then fifty-two-year-old Browning, and pretty soon the pair had people all over New York City gossiping about their May-December romance (or maybe it was *March*-December). Decency leagues and New York child protection agencies were throwing some serious heat at their relationship. Under that kind of pressure, what could Browning do? He married her.

As it turns out, the age difference may have been the least strange part of their relationship. The two lived with "Daddy's" pet African goose, which Peaches complained about because it honked all day, and with Peaches's mother, whom Browning complained about because she sometimes slept in their bedroom.

In 1926, tired of all the controversy swirling around him and his child bride, Browning decided to flee New York and bring Peaches and her armful of new diamond and platinum bracelets to the relatively cool, relaxed surroundings of Manchester, Vermont. Naturally, they stayed at the Equinox.

Imagine the picture they must have made: a filthy rich and awfully peculiar middle-aged real estate developer and his own personal nymphet. Congressman Adam Clayton Powell Jr. worked at the Equinox the summer of 1926 as a bellhop. He recalled that the couple brought along *twenty-six* pieces of luggage. He said it took an entire day for them to unload and unpack it all. I wonder if some of them were full of the "dirty French magazines" Peaches later claimed her husband made her look at.

Daddy left the tip to Peaches, giving her a $100 bill and instructing her to pass it along to the young men. Fortunately for them, they'd seen the money before Browning left the room. Once he was gone, Peaches tried to distract the boys. She opened her robe, giving them a good look at her voluptuous form while attempting to pass off a ten-spot. They caught her at her game and managed to talk her into forking over the full $100. I hope it made up for the mess that goose must have made. I've read that he brought it everywhere, even taking it along on his and Peaches's honeymoon.

Daddy and Peaches with their African goose. *Courtesy the Library of Congress.*

Even with the goose, a small tip wouldn't have bothered me if I could have only gotten a glimpse of Browning doing something Peaches complained about in court after their fairy tale finally fractured. She said when they were alone, he would run around their apartment nude, on all fours, barking like a German shepherd. Every time I think of it, I burst out laughing, and that's something money can't buy.

Here's an interesting tidbit. Remember the scene in John Hughes's *The Breakfast Club* in which Vernon, the bitter weekend detention teacher, is talking to Carl, the custodian, about their youthful dreams and expectations? It goes like this:

> *Vernon: What did you want to be when you were young?*
> *Carl: When I was a kid, I wanted to be John Lennon.*
> *Vernon: Carl, don't be a goof. I'm trying to make a serious point here.*

The phrase "Don't be a goof" was coined by Edward Browning. Wikipedia says that it was an admonishment he used to put Peaches in her place. The insult caught on, turning up in the lyrics of the song "On Your Toes" in the musical of the same name by Rodgers and Hart.

BIBLIOGRAPHY

Allen, Richard. "The Connection Between Two Williston Crimes." *Williston Observer,* June 16, 2011.

Allen Family Papers, Special Collections, University of Vermont.

Bendici, Ray. *Speaking Ill of the Dead: Jerks in Connecticut History.* N.p.: Morris Book Publishing, 2012.

The Breakfast Club. Directed by John Hughes. A&M Films, 1985, distributed by Universal Pictures.

Burlington Free Press. "Beware of Bootleg Liquor." January 1920.

———. "Bloodhounds Sent Home." August 3, 1908.

———. "Catherine Driscoll Dillon, Obituary." January 11, 1872.

———. "Confession, Pitezel." April 13 1896.

———. "Conviction of Forgers." October 30, 1854.

———. "Den Stone Circus." June 22, 1868.

———. "Foul Murder in East Wallingford." July 25, 1908.

———. "The Griswold Murder." April 10, 1866; April 13–14, 1866; April 20, 1866.

———. "The Griswold Murder." October 2, 1868.

———. "The Griswold Murder." September 8, 1865.

———. "Horrible Murder—Wife Chloroformed Him." August 16, 1902.

———. "Humors of the Vermont AAPA and Women's Aid." June 6, 1929. http://burlingtonfreepress.newspapers.com/image/197323685/?terms=Speakeasy%2BWinooski.

———. "Land on Which Todd's Home Is Built Will Not Be Taxed until 2807." February 3, 1951.

———. "Long Murder Case Appealed." October 18, 1921.

———. "Mildred Brewster Case Before the Grand Jury." October 6, 1897.

———. "Miss Brewster Better." June 4, 1897.

———. "Mrs. Broadwell's Body Exhumed." June 3, 1919.

———. "Mrs. Parker and Long Indicted." June 11, 1919.

———. "Outsiders Strain for Acceptance." April 25, 1999.

———. "Petition for Divorce." November 5, 1858.

———. "Potter Case." October 2, 1868.

———. "Potter Case." October 3, 1866.

———. "Shot Her Rival in Love." May 31, 1897.

———. "Special, Winooski Is Innocent." August 7, 1908.

———. "Stone and Murray's Circus." May 15, 1868.

———. "Suspect Kent Is Murderer." July 27, 1908.

———. "Tax Sale." January 8, 1856.

———. "Three Sentenced for Liquor Sales." November 26, 1946. http:// burlingtonfreepress.newspapers.com/image/199268487/?terms=Dorot hy%2BO'Leary.

———. "Timothy Follett's Estate." April 3, 1857.

———. "Twenty Seven Years on the Docket." May 11, 1878.

———. "Vice Quiz Ends with No Charges Against Davies." July 22, 1961. http://burlingtonfreepress.newspapers.com/image/200237113/?terms =Ed%2BDavies.

———. "Will Be Tried for Murder." July 20, 1895.

Buzzfeed. "Presidential Facial Hair Power Ranking: The Moustaches of Western Civilization." https://www.buzzfeed.com/bennyjohnson/ presidential-facial-hair-power-ranking?utm_term=.jtGJ1rxkg#. dsRXQ4Kqr.

CBS News. "The Original Birther Controversy." November 5, 2012. www. cbsnews.com/news/the-original-birther-controversy.

Chester Alan Arthur Papers, Library of Congress.

Cortisson, Ellen Mackay Hutchinson, and Edmund Clarence Stedman, comps. and eds. *A Library of American Literature*. Vol. 3. N.p.: Charles L. Webster and Company, 1892.

Crockett, Walter Hill. *A History of Lake Champlain: The Record of Three Centuries, 1609–1909*. Burlington, VT: McAuliffe Paper Company, 1937.

A Dude a Day. "Our 'Dude Presidents'—'Chet' Arthur and 'Teddy' Roosevelt." http://a-dude-a-day.blogspot.com/2016/02/our-dude-presidents-chet-arthur-and.html.

Duffy, John J., and H. Nicholas Muller III. *Inventing Ethan Allen.* Lebanon, NH: University Press of New England, 2014.

Duffy, John J., Samuel B. Hand and Ralph H. Orth. "Fairfield." *The Vermont Encyclopedia.* Lebanon, NH: University of Vermont Press, 2003.

Ethan Allen Homestead. www.ethanallenhomestead.org.

GQ. "The Official Power Ranking of American Presidential Facial Hair." https://www.gq.com/gallery/american-presidents-with-facial-hair.

Greenburg, Michael. *Peaches and Daddy.* New York: Overlook Press, 2008.

Hemenway, Abby Maria. *Vermont Historical Gazetteer* 3 (1877).

History. "Mother's Day." http://www.history.com/topics/holidays/mothers-day.

The Illustrated American 15 (1894).

Kaelber, Lutz. Eugenics: Compulsory Sterilization in 50 American States. University of Vermont, 2012. http://www.uvm.edu/~lkaelber/eugenics/VT/VT.html.

Kasper, Shirl. *Annie Oakley.* Norman: University of Oklahoma Press, 1992.

Krakowsi, Adam. *Vermont Prohibition: Teetotalers, Bootleggers & Corruption.* Charleston, SC: The History Press, May 16, 2016.

Larson, Erik. *Devil in the White City: Murder, Magic and Madness at the Fair that Changed America.* New York: Vintage Books, 2004.

Laskow, Sarah. "The Gilded Age's Only Female Tycoon Lived in Brooklyn to Avoid Taxes." Atlas Obscura, May 27, 2015. http://www.atlasobscura.com/articles/hetty-green-gilded-age-female-tycoon-brooklyn.

The Lawyers Reports. Annotated. Rochester, NY: Lawyers Cooperative Publishing Company, 1910.

Lee, Dan P. "Peaches: Who's Your Daddy?" *New York Magazine,* April 1, 2012. http://nymag.com/news/features/scandals/peaches-browning-2012-4.

Lewis, Thea. *Haunted Burlington: Spirits of Vermont's Queen City.* Charleston, SC: The History Press, 2009.

———. *Haunted Inns and Ghostly Getaways of Vermont.* Charleston, SC: The History Press, 2014.

Los Angeles Times. "A Hard Cider and Bourbon Cocktail for the Holiday Season." December 21, 2015.

Markel, Dr. Howard. "The Dirty, Painful Death of President James A. Garfield." PBS, September 16, 2016. http://www.pbs.org/newshour/updates/dirty-painful-death-president-james-garfield.

McGuire, Gregory. *Wicked: The Life and Times of the Wicked Witch of the West.* New York: HarperCollins, 1995.

Miller, Edward, and Frederick Wells. *A History of Ryegate, Vermont: From Its Settlement by the Scotch-American Company of Farmers to Present Time, with Genealogical Records of Many Families*. St. Johnsbury, VT: Caledonian Company, 1913.

Mills, Cynthia. Vermont Historical Society. https://vermonthistory.org/journal/68/vt681_203.pdf.

Mitchell, Sarah E. "Louis Comfort Tiffany's Work on the White House." Vintage Designs, 2003. http://vintagedesigns.com/fam/wh/tiff/index.htm.

New England Historical Society. "Another Look at Hetty Green, the Witch of Wall Street." http://www.newenglandhistoricalsociety.com/another-look-hetty-green-witch-wall-street.

———. "Mary Rogers Brings the Capital Punishment Wars to Vermont." http://www.newenglandhistoricalsociety.com/mary-rogers-brings-the-capital-punishment-wars-to-vermont.

———. "Queen Lill Made Vermont Famous—for Booze and Broads." http://www.newenglandhistoricalsociety.com/queen-lill-made-vermont-famous-booze-broads.

———. "Six Historic Wealthy Enclaves…and the Scandals They Spawned." http://www.newenglandhistoricalsociety.com/six-historic-wealthy-enclaves-scandals-spawned.

New York Times. "Horrible Murder in Vermont: Tragedy at Williston." September 3, 1865.

O'Neil, Daniel. "Uncoiling the Black Snake Affair." *Burlington Free Press*, September 25, 2014. www.burlingtonfreepress.com.

Palmer, Mary Tyler, "An American Matron." *The Maternal Physician: A Treatise on the Nurture and Management of Infants, from the Birth until Two Years Old*. N.p.: Isaac Riley, Publisher, 1811.

Plummer, Todd. "A Craft Beer Crawl through Burlington, Vermont." *Vogue*, May 9, 2017. http://www.vogue.com/article/burlington-vermont-craft-beer-crawl.

Powell, Adam Clayton, Jr. *Adam by Adam: The Autobiography of Adam Clayton Powell Jr*. USA: Kensington Publishing, 1994.

Ramsey, Connie Cain. "The Ghost of Montpelier's Courthouse." *Burlington Free Press*, November 6, 2014. http://www.burlingtonfreepress.com/story/news/local/2014/11/06/ghost-montpeliers-courthouse/18605573.

REMAX North Professionals. "Vermont's Haunted Homes." November 2, 2015. www.homesvermont.com/blog/vermonts-haunted-homes.html.

Robinson, Helen Marvin. "Dream Lake." *The Vermonter* 23.

Royall Tyler Online. "The Contrast." November 20, 2012. https://qapuitem.jimdo.com/2012/11/20/the-contrast-royall-tyler-online.

San Francisco Call. "Mary Rogers Ready to Die." January 30, 1905.

Schechter, Harold. *Depraved: The Definitive True Story of H.H. Holmes, Whose Grotesque Crimes Shattered Turn-of-the-Century Chicago.* N.p.: Pocket Books, 1994.

Seeking the Phoenix. "Judge Royall Tyler in the House of the Seven Gables." http://www.geocities.ws/seekingthephoenix/t/judgeroyalltyler.htm.

Shattuck, Gary. "Biggest Jerk of the Revolution?" All Things Liberty. allthingsliberty.com.

Singer, Michelle. "The Bridge: The True Story Behind the Legend of Anna's Ghost." *The Bridge*, November 4, 2015. http://www.montpelierbridge.com/2015/10/the-true-story-behind-the-legend-of-annas-ghost.

Slout, William. "Olympians of the Sawdust Circle." *Borgo Press*, 1988.

Snopes. "Black Agnes." http://www.snopes.com/horrors/ghosts/agnes.asp.

State of Vermont Historic Sites. "Chester Arthur." http://historicsites.vermont.gov/directory/arthur.

St. John, Thomas. "A Chapter from 'Nathaniel Hawthorne: Studies in the House of the Seven Gables.'" Nathaniel Hawthorne: Studies in the House of the Seven Gables. http://hawthornessevengables.com

Sutherland, Pete. "The Black Snake and The Fly." Freedom and Unity, 1992. freedomandunity.org.

Terrell, Ellen. "But Was She Really the 'Witch of Wall Street'?" Library of Congress, March 14, 2012. https://blogs.loc.gov/inside_adams/2012/03/but-was-she-really-the-witch-of-wall-street.

Thayer, Stuart, and William L. Slout. "American Circus Anthology: Essays of the Early Years." Circus Historical Society. http://www.circushistory.org/Thayer/Thayer3m.htm.

Town of Wallingford, Vermont. "Murder on Sugar Hill." http://www.wallingfordvt.com/wp-content/uploads/2014/07/Murder-on-Sugar-Hill.pdf.

Township of Nutley, New Jersey. "History of Nutley." http://www.nutleynj.org/history-of-nutley.

UVM Historic Preservation Program. http://www.uvm.edu/histpres/HPJ/burl1830/streets/king/35king.html.

Vermont Deadline. "Awful and Naughty in Richford." http://vermontdeadline.blogspot.com/2014/11/awful-and-naughty-richford.html.

———. "Oh, Mercie." http://vermontdeadline.blogspot.com/2013/09/oh-mercie.html.

Vermont Eugenics: A Documentary History. University of Vermont. http://www.uvm.edu/~eugenics.

Vermont Folklore, Myths, Legends, Ghost Stories and More. "Vermont Ghosts or Nonsense? The Hayden Family Curse—Albany, VT." Vermonter.com.

Vermont Historical Society 38, no. 1 (1970). vermonthistory.org.

Vermont Historical Society. "Black Snake Affair Papers, 1805–1809." MSA 263. www.vermonthistory.org.

———. "Ethan Allen: Vermont History Explorer." https://vermonthistory.org/explorer/people-places/whos-who/famous-vermonters/ethan-allen.

———. "A Guide to the Royall Tyler Collection." 1995. http://vermonthistory.org/documents/findaid/tyler.pdf.

———. "Hetty Howland Robinson Green." http://vermonthistory.org/research/vermont-women-s-history/database/green-hetty.

———. "Mary Rogers." http://vermonthistory.org/research/vermont-women-s-history/database/rogers-mary.

———. "Prohibition." http://vermonthistory.org/research/research-resources-online/green-mountain-chronicles/prohibition-1920.

Vermont's Bolton War. http://www.vermontsboltonwar.com/?page_id=33.

Wheeler, Scott. "Bootlegging in Vermont Was Risky Business." Vermonter. http://vermonter.com/bootlegging-vermont.

The White House. "Chester Arthur." https://www.whitehouse.gov/about-the-white-house/presidents/chester-a-arthur/

Wikipedia. "Emeline Meaker." https://en.wikipedia.org/wiki/Emeline_Meaker.

———. "Ethan Allen." www.wikipedia.org.

———. "Hetty Green." https://en.wikipedia.org/wiki/Hetty_Green.

———. "Lucina Broadwell." https://en.wikipedia.org/wiki/Lucina_C._Broadwell.

———. "Maine Law." https://en.wikipedia.org/wiki/Maine_law.

———. "Peaches Browning." https://en.wikipedia.org/wiki/Peaches_Browning.

———. "Royall Tyler." https://en.wikipedia.org/wiki/Royall_Tyler.

———. "William Hayden House, Albany Vermont." https://en.wikipedia.org/wiki/William_Hayden_House_(Albany,_Vermont).

Williston Observer. "Hints of Horrors Haunt Williston." October 5, 2005.

Young, Joanna Tebbs. "Vermont Eugenics: When Our Branding Wasn't So Sweet." *Rutland Reader*. February 19, 2014.

INDEX

Burlington Free Press 84
Burlington High School 102
Burlington, Vermont 10, 66, 115, 128

C

Canada 12, 18, 19, 20, 27, 42, 45, 46, 60, 64, 65, 72, 74, 75, 118
Capone, Al 45
Chadwick, William 30
Chittenden County Correctional Center 49
Clark, Charles Edgar 137
Cleveland, Manning 84
Clifford, Elizabeth Gilmore 98
Clifford, Eugene 98
Coles, Ira 53
Cole, William H. 53
Collamer, Jacob 9
Congdon, Delia 81
Congdon, James Headley 81
Conkling, Roscoe 74
Curtis, A.B. 122
Cutting, Amos P. 90

D

Dale, Mercie 26
"Dead Man's Shuffle" 117, 120
Dean, Cyrus 21
Dickens, Charles 71
Dillon, Patrick 42
Dow, Eva 124
Dow, Neal 41
Driscoll, Catherine Dillon 42
Druid Ridge Cemetery 92

Dunder, Rock 84
Duskie, Elizabeth 48
Duxbury 95

E

Eaton, Sarah 51
Equinox Hotel 143
eugenics 138, 139, 140, 141, 142

F

Fitch, John 68
Flannagan, Noble B. 62
Follett, Timothy 67
Foster, Stephen 64
Fulton, Robert 68

G

Galton, Sir Francis 138, 140
Garfield, James A. 72, 74
Gill, John 129
Goodenough, John F. 103
Graham, Elizabeth Jennings 73
Grant, Ulysses S. 74
Green, Edward Henry 111
Green, Harriet Sylvia Ann Howland 112
Green, Hetty 109
Green Mountain Boys 10, 12, 13
Green Mountain Patriot 40
Griswold, Ephraim 60, 63
Griswold, Sally 60
Grout, D.D. 86

ABOUT THE AUTHOR

*A*uthor and historian Thea Lewis is a Vermont native and the creator of Queen City Ghostwalk, the walking tour chosen "Best Scary Stroll" by *Yankee* magazine. Known as Vermont's Queen of Halloween, she's been scaring up history since 2002 with her haunted tours, special events and books for adults and children. Thea's other titles with The History Press include *Haunted Burlington: Spirits of Vermont's Queen City, Ghosts and Legends of Lake Champlain* and *Haunted Inns and Ghostly Getaways of Vermont*.